Revelations

on

The Book of Revelation

WINIFRED MacCARDELL FLOOD

with a new Introduction by
Christa Phillips

LivingSpring Publishing
Roundup, Montana
2016

Living Spring website: http://living- spring.org/cms/en/living-spring/

Published by:
LivingSpring Publishing
Roundup, MT 59072
406-323-2465

Designed, and cover photo, by: Michelle Clement

Library of Congress Preassigned Control Number: **2016958228**
Revelations on The Book of Revelation / Winifred MacCardell Flood; New Introduction by Christa Phillips
Reprint: December 2016; Originally published: December 1953

ISBN, paperback: 978-0-9852910-0-6
ISBN, ePub e-book: 978-0-9852910-2-0

Printed in the United States of America by IngramSpark

3 5 7 9 10 8 6 4 2

Review (continued from back cover)

The Book of Revelation has far too long been treated as a strange and foreboding book filled with dire prophecy. Mrs. Flood declares that the great book is prophesying but not in the sense that such and such a war shall come to pass in this year or that . . . that depressions and desolation will occur in this or that time. Rather, she tells us, it is saying in every chapter and verse that "the calamity in your mind, the depression in your soul, the war in your spirit *must express in your life* and in your world as physical, mental and spiritual desolation."

This interpretation holds that the allegorical writings of the original have been set down in code, so to speak, not to hide from us but to preserve for us the Eternal Truths which man so carelessly overlooks. The great original, she states, says over and over that there is only One Power in the universe and that each one uses that power constantly and inevitably; how one uses it, and for what purpose, will decide his failure or success, his discontent or happiness.

I find this a book well worth reading, pondering and studying in all humility. There is an amazing truth herein revealed, a truth which can lead to the discovery of the True Self, can lead to a better philosophy of life, and that fuller, more joyous and abundant life for which all mankind seeks.

—Laura M. Hyer, D.S.B., review in *Winter Park Topics*, February 26, 1954

Table of Contents

Introduction to the New Edition v
Preface viii
Foreword xi
Chapter 1 1
Chapter 2 5
Chapter 3 10
Chapter 4 15
Chapter 5 18
Chapter 6 22
Chapter 7 26
Chapter 8 30
Chapter 9 33
Chapter 10 38
Chapter 11 42
Chapter 12 48
Chapter 13 53
Chapter 14 59
Chapter 15 65
Chapter 16 67
Chapter 17 73
Chapter 18 78
Chapter 19 84
Chapter 20 90
Chapter 21 94
Chapter 22 102

Introduction to the New Edition

COMING ACROSS *Revelations on The Book of Revelation* by Winifred MacCardell Flood has been one of the great miracles in my life. It had been in my late husband's library unnoticed by me for decades, had been moved various times across New York City and twice across the ocean. Every time I had been the packer, unconscious of its presence. When it found me—and I have to word it this way for I was not looking for it—I was living in Virginia Beach at Community House, a house for spiritual teaching and healing, which together with a circle of friends I had founded in 1989. I have no explanation other than that divine providence caused me to climb on that chair in front of the bookshelf one day in 1994 and reach for just this book. I don't remember searching for anything in particular or pondering any deep questions that day. But—almost witnessing this as a bystander—I felt myself reach up, draw this worn, thin little book out from the row of others, and step off the chair somewhat dumbfounded. When I opened the book and began to read, I knew I had been handed a great gift. I sat down and read and read for hours, again and again taking my eyes off the book to ponder what I had read and heard through the words. My heart was deeply touched as hardly ever before.

I had been exposed to Christian teaching all through my childhood as I was raised in a Christian family and community. My parents were both strong believers and—what I considered a real blessing—they loved God and Jesus with all their heart. I know this from the reading, singing, and prayers that I as a child of seven experienced in our family every day at all meals and also at bedtime. Whenever we encountered problems they were dealt with in the presence of God, in prayer and guidance that made Him the Source of all Good. Grace as the source of our experiencing healthy lives was undisputed and so was the need to express gratitude at all times. Of course, our "Christian Life" also had its drawbacks for us growing up. There were rules and interpretations of the Word at times worse than Paul could have given them during his severest

Revelations on The Book of Revelation

struggles and most narrow-mindedness. For example, at seven years old I was not allowed to join a children's athletics course (an ungodly place to go), and for the same reason none of us was allowed to learn to dance.

Being a Bible reader since childhood, the book of Revelation has held—as for most people probably—an intriguing fascination for me. But I did not understand its doomsday prophecy. It was difficult for me to comprehend that an all-loving and generous God would give such to mankind. "My" God was different, I decided. So, as a young adult, I began to struggle with church teaching and interpretation, mistrusted the Word's interpretation by theologians and laypeople alike, whom I saw as not living according to their proclamations, talking of Love and an all-giving Father, but acting on fear and desire for self-preservation. Despite my struggle with the Christian establishment, I maintained my love for God, and Jesus continued to be the Special Presence in my life. However, I also became an avid searcher and student of the teachings of Truth in a wide spectrum of philosophy and thereby became also acquainted with the teachings of other world religions. I am deeply grateful for my path and the many opportunities that I encountered. For I understand today that all religions are resting in the covenant of God with man and that all paths are leading to the One. I have become aware that Jesus did not come to create a religion (and definitely not the many forms of churches that have developed since), but to lead us beyond it and through the door.

Years prior to my finding the book *Revelations on The Book of Revelation* by MacCardell Flood, I came across some very interesting readings given by Edgar Cayce,[1] the American clairvoyant, on various spiritual subjects among which were the Life of Jesus and the Book of Revelation. My heart rejoiced for I had come across profound wisdom—all that had seemed so puzzling now suddenly made sense. What struck me most was the impact this "prophecy" and guidance had on my personal life! It was as though

---

1 The Association for Research and Enlightenment (A.R.E.) holds all transcripts of the readings given by Edgar Cayce. A great wealth of information containing areas such as the medical, mental, emotional, religious, cultural, past lives, and personal is available to the public. Much of it has also been published in books. The ARE is at 67th and Atlantic Avenue, Virginia Beach, VA 23451.

Introduction

shades were taken off my eyes and vision was restored, a vision in which the heart felt totally at home. So perhaps this, too, had prepared me in a way for opening this Book by Winifred MacCardell Flood.

If *Revelations on The Book of Revelation* fell into your hands, you can rest assured it is by providence. You probably are gifted with a seeker's open mind and aware that God's revelation has never been limited to certain centuries or certain religious avenues. But it has been an ongoing activity of His Holy Spirit offered in the continuous Grace to those willing to seek and find, ask and listen. It is by that same Grace that the senses of our heart are awakened and enabled to perceive Truth and also recognize the unconditional Love with which it comes. Therefore, I have nothing to add to the brief Foreword by Winifred MacCardell Flood. It says it all. And to interpret or discourse on the content of the book itself seems to be a trespass, which I feel not invited to do.

Revelations on The Book of Revelation has been out of print for years, and, as far as I was able to ascertain, cannot be found any longer in any bookstore. This fact and my deep gratitude for the living food this book contains have created a strong desire in me to re-publish it and make it available again to those hungry for deeper understanding and to those, perhaps even hungrier, for becoming whole and healed. May it serve the purpose that all Teachings of Truth have served through the ages to lead you back home.

Not much more is to be said. I have maintained the original text for re-publishing, including all Italics by the author contained therein. However, the spelling of a few words was brought up-to-date, and a few punctuation marks were added or changed where they seemed appropriate.

I am deeply grateful to Michelle Clement for being willing to take the actual task of re-publishing under her competent and persevering wing and creating the book that *Revelations on The Book of Revelation* has now become.

Christa Phillips
Living Spring, Montana
November 2016

Preface

IT MAY BE of interest to the reader to know the method by which I worked to arrive at this entirely new interpretation of the so-puzzling and so misunderstood Book of Revelation.

Using the Hebrew and Greek Dictionary in *Strong's Exhaustive Concordance* I have traced the King James words through every reference given and compiled a file of all possible meanings for each word.

In interpreting each Verse I have laid before me the file cards on each word in that Verse and have tried to select those words and meanings which most nearly reveal a God of Love; a plan for growth and unfoldment; a picture of that through which we all go, i.e. ups and downs, fear and courage, hope and despair, etc.

All 22 Chapters of the Book of Revelation are graphic descriptions of the extreme vacillation of man's feelings—the tug of war which goes on as he reaches for his Divinity and then becomes discouraged at not attaining it at once—this occurs

OVER AND OVER AND OVER AGAIN.

To best understand this book it would be wise to read it through the first time with the King James Version in hand—alternate verse by corresponding verse.

For example: *Chap.* 12, *verse* 4: *of* KING JAMES

And his tail drew the third part of the stars of heaven, and did cast them to the earth: and the dragon stood before the woman that was ready to be delivered, for to devour her child as soon as it was born.

Preface

REVISED STANDARD (*same verse*)

His tail *swept down* a third of the stars of heaven, and cast them to the earth: and the dragon stood before the woman who was *about to bear* a child, that he might devour her child when she brought it forth.

WORDS LOOKED UP:
Tail: cut off,
Third: intensify,
Part: separate,
Deliver: strengthen,
Star: shining, luminous,
Heaven: exalted or expansion,
Earth: opposite, opposition, in the sense of heaven being *invisible* (in its power of expansion) and earth being *visible* (the opposite in expression),
Dragon: monster to destroy or weaken,
Child: idea,
Stand: confirm,
Ready: prepare,
Born: bring forth.

TRANSLATION

The feeling of being "*cut-off*" (*intense* separation) from the Father—or *goodness itself*—gives just as great and *intense* a feeling of *separation* as the opposite gives of unity. *Cut-off* from the ability to cause good is the greatest destruction possible and is even as a *monster* looming up in *opposition* and *confirming* aloneness. Be prepared for this dual possibility, be not afraid of the undesirable but be steadfast in considering the desirable. Be diligent in expectation of only Good, *strengthen* your belief and *desire earnestly* to live true to the Highest *Idea* you can *bring forth* and you will beget or produce a Savior.

THROUGHOUT THE BOOK is this type of translation—not an evaluation by me as to my opinion of what might or should be

Revelations on The Book of Revelation

found. I emphasize this point because, being a translation from English into English, one is less conscious of the idea of TRANSLATION. I am actually translating original Hebrew root-words while endeavoring to keep the Biblical flavor and rhythm and style. I have not tried to interject a personal evaluation or interpretation of the words as they came from this original. The language, sometimes, may seem a little stilted but I have tried to keep the flow of the wordage as it interpreted itself to me.

Foreword

THERE IS A POWER which men use constantly, for life and health or for decay and death. This is the message of the Book of Revelation.

The Book of Revelation has been treated as a strange, a foreboding, a weird book. Men have tried to make it into a dire prophecy, foreseeing for the physical planet and its people all manner of doom as inescapable and vengeful fate.

It *is* prophesying but it is not saying that such and such a war shall come to pass in this year or that; it is not saying that depressions and desolations are to appear at this time or in that era.

It is saying, rather, in every chapter and verse, that the calamity in your mind, the depression in your soul, the war in your spirit must express in your life and in your world as physical, mental and spiritual desolation. It is saying that *as you use* the power so freely given you—even so must that power express.

In Isaiah 45 and Lord God says: I AM THE LORD AND THERE IS NONE ELSE. . . . I FORM THE LIGHT AND CREATE DARKNESS, I MAKE PEACE AND CREATE EVIL . . . and CONCERNING THE WORK OF MY HANDS COMMAND YE ME . . . THERE IS NO GOD ELSE BESIDE ME, A JUST GOD AND A SAVIOR. . . . LOOK UNTO ME AND BE YE SAVED. . . . FOR I AM GOD, AND THERE IS NONE ELSE.

This great Book of Revelation is reiterating these statements, it is saying there is no other power in the universe! Each one uses this power constantly and inevitably, and as he uses it he experiences calamity, depression, war—or delivery, success, peace.

We have become used to stories of espionage and intrigue and to the fact that allied countries send important messages to one another in code. We know that to understand the vital message the words must be de-coded, that there is a key which reveals the true meaning behind the appearing words. The vital truth is preserved *from* the enemy or the careless one and is preserved *for* those who are in accord with the sender.

Just so this ageless and mystical collection of Truths—the Bible—is come to us in CODE. Its message is hidden—not to keep *from* us but to preserve *for* us. The key is in the fact that *vital* words are words which *can mean many things*. Taking the words at their face value the stories and incidents are merely interesting or exciting or even shocking: Decoding the words, tracing them back to their original state we often find that a given word might have meant from two to twenty-two differing things in the days in which these stories were originally told.

Every word in this interpretation is a legitimate word: that is to say the word found in the King James version is but *one* possible meaning of the original word which was translated into the English version. Trying to read words only as those words are used today limits our understanding and keeps us in bondage to outer things and to fear. Studying the other permissible and *perfectly legitimate meanings* we find that the whole Bible is endeavoring to enrich our lives—to free us from fear—to reveal to us the Power which is in each one of us to be used by each one of us for ever-increasing good. WE DO USE THIS POWER—WE USE IT DAILY, CONSTANTLY—THERE IS NOTHING ELSE FOR US TO USE, *EXCEPT THE POWER*. How we use it, for what purpose we use it—upon this depends our failure or success, our discontent or our happiness.

It is to teach us the right use of this inner power that this REVELATION was written.

Chapter 1

VERSE 1

The medium by which God reveals hidden knowledge, and furnishes that which is needed, is Realization of the Saving Power of SELF-KNOWLEDGE. "He will save" (Christ Jesus, not as a man, but as "realization" of "inner power"—this is the "light that lighteth every man that cometh into the world," that which is implanted in every man at birth). This it is which God (that which causes to be) gave unto man to show to all who will bring forth from within themselves, things which must come to pass as this knowledge is used. God revealed this by a messenger—a sign—to John, (THE SELF-EXISTENT SELF).

VERSE 2

Thus this revelation will be clear only to those who *do* recognize their Self-existence. Such ones are indeed blessed or given increase of knowledge.

VERSE 3

Both those who read and those who hear the words and *all* that the words mean are blessed (hear and see in the sense of inner perception) for the "time is at hand" for all who are willing to understand.

VERSE 4

John, The Self-Existent Self, communicates to the seven churches—to the completed ones at that point whence new action is about to move—communicates to them at the principle, ruling or commencing point: joy be unto you and new completion, may you set-at-one-again your Self and your Desire. This message comes to you from the One and Only, the Everlasting One—from that complete and perfect breath of life which is a gift from God and which has the power to bring to you all things.

Revelations on The Book of Revelation

VERSE 5

Also from Jesus Christ (the saving power within, realized for what it is—which in and of itself testifies to the truth of all this)—from Jesus Christ, the first-begotten of the dead or that which follows letting go of old unwanted things, hear this: you *must* die-for-the-son, i.e. give up your life as father-mother to bring forth or become the child, the new idea. *This*, this inner self-knowing, is the greatest of the rulers of the earth.

VERSE 6

Let us give prominence and splendor and power to this one that has clung to us, stayed with us, taken away our sense of separation by the very life-giving force of Being and so made us kings and priests unto Goodness. Surely you can see this—firmly—truly: *IT IS*.

VERSE 7

Look intently and with joy for this great revelation comes as a densely-appearing, a difficult-to-perceive, essence; but it is a firmament, a strong, sure, firm reality if you can see it so! All that look may perceive and be content, even those which sought to destroy and revile this revelation. Even so all similar reactions to this truth may cause lamentations because Its power is one that brings to pass according to the acceptance. So shall it be strong and firm in joy *or* sorrow.

VERSE 8

I am Alpha, the first cause, which is of change; without this first causative state there could only be privation, but *WITH* it is union—a uniting to the new which permits me to pass on from the former state to become that which also I am, Omega, the finality. Thus am I the beginning, the original, the first or principle; and the infinite, never-ending goal; for I am the very uttermost future perfection. I am the opening idea for change, I am the change itself, and I am the resulting completion: eternity expressing, I the

Chapter 1

Universal Law, the Absolute One, that was, that is and that ever shall be. *I AM IT*.

VERSE 9

I, John, the Self-Existent one, through the unifying force of love am also one with you, co-participant in your trouble and in the foundation and endurance of this revelation. I was in that longing state (*isle*) awaiting the idea of Goodness and the evidence of saving power.

VERSE 10

I was in the inside—the center of my being—on that day or time of perfect rest and I heard the sacred name as a vibration within me,

VERSE 11

saying: I am the One—first Cause and final reward. That which unrolls from your inner Consciousness engrave and arrange that you may declare it unto an indefinite number of meeting places, that you may call out, from the inner starting point or cause, these truths. Declare the Truth to: (1) those who discover and find, (2) those who are embittered, (3) those who are fortified by reason of having ascertained or "dug it out" for themselves, (4) those who have sacrificed one idea for a better one, (5) those who have trembled but still found strength, (6) those who feel close to mankind, and (7) those who stand for true justice. To all these declare the Truth that I, the Mighty One within themselves, am the Alpha and Omega—the Cause which starts and completes every idea.

VERSE 12

And I, John, turned to verify the authority by contact and thus perceived the complete, pure beam, the shining illumination.

VERSE 13

In the midst of this shining purity stood the Perfect One, wrapped in the splendor of justice, victorious, all swelling of human insolence or intolerance restrained with purity,

Revelations on The Book of Revelation

VERSE 14
dedicated, set apart in dazzling whiteness, his vision gleaming and a-fire as with lightning;

VERSE 15
of radiant understanding (feet) the very foundation of all justice. The sound of this Perfect One was as the sound of much excellence, and revealed that all falseness *could be refined and subjugated by joining with it.*

VERSE 16
In the integrity of this Power was complete luminosity, joy and intelligence, the ability to show or make known the way; and out of his speech came the pointed, gleaming, two-edged *word*; and his appearance was dazzlingly bright, shining as firm courageous power.

VERSE 17
When I sensed this Real Self to be in me I relaxed to my own personal impotency and the Real Self placed a verdict upon me and said: Abide in my power, with reverence, for *I am all*, I am both the Original Cause and the final appearance.

VERSE 18
I am your future, I am the present state of existence that becoming relaxed, looses the appearance and behold, shows a new appearance. I Am that which was, that which is and that which ever shall be—ALL—and ALL NOW. This is sure: it is I who both open and close the sense state of limitation and pestilence.

VERSE 19
Engrave all this deep in yourself consciously!

VERSE 20
All of this is engraved within, a mystery, till you again *and from your own desire* go within to uncover and reveal the truth.

Chapter 2

VERSE 1

To the driving force at the originating centers of those who are discovering their real selves (Ephesus), declare: that the one who holds complete luminosity in the firm integrity of his approach and power, who moves, radiating the pure beam,

VERSE 2

that that one is aware of what they are doing and of their endurance in the doing, but is also aware that they are unable to put up with those who do otherwise! I am aware of their efforts to search out the assertions of those who claim to be ambassadors of Christ but whom they discover not to be.

VERSE 3

I have watched them struggling along and sticking to the cause;

VERSE 4

but for all their efforts I am not pleased because they have ceased clinging to the original choice [by implication this original choice is that one of caring-for-the-Truth-regardless-of-what-any-one-else-does-or-thinks-about-it]. This choice they have abandoned.

VERSE 5

To these hardy ones I suggest a return to that first high state of perception, and that they act according to that initial realization, else they will find that soon the beam, the pure illumination of the joy of Truth, will fade for them.

VERSE 6

There is, however, one thing that these persevering, discovering ones have: they persecute and push away the *deeds* of the opposition force, against which I too am opposed.

VERSE 7

Let him that heareth perceive inwardly what the breath of life says at the fountain-head! Hear this: To the one that rises over his fears and his doubts will I give the sense of that firm state of existence which is in the midst of the orchard of Goodness.

VERSE 8

And to that center aspect of bitterness (Smyrna) declare: the Original Cause, which is also the Final Appearance (the state which loosed its hold upon the false appearance and is refreshed in a true state of vitality):

VERSE 9

declare to that one that I, the Original Cause, from this new state, am aware of your endeavor to change, of your sense of trouble and lack (but in very truth you *are* abundantly supplied, no matter how it seems to you). I also understand the sting in the vilification of those who are claiming to be searching for God more than they admit that you are, although they are not so at all. [Satan is only your feeling of the impossibility of attaining your high desire.]

VERSE 10

Turn aside from none of these things which come upon you, even of seeming pain; for look you, this *sense* of opposition shall limit some of you only that you may learn. It is true that you shall be in a tight place for an accumulation of days, but stay calm until you can loose—or drop—the sense of fear and I will reward you with the new state of existence!

VERSE 11

Listen well, for when you get the meaning of this you will no longer be hurt by this reasoning.

VERSE 12

And to those who are fortified by reason of having "dug it out," or ascertained for themselves (Pergamus) declare: these are the

Chapter 2

things to be found in words—two sides—two meanings—look well, that you resolve them to one point!

VERSE 13

I know that your acts and your words do not always agree, that you claim me for your strength and declare your faith in me even while you appear to release your opposition thoughts. You accuse yourself and slay—rather than resolve your opposing ideas to the complete one.

VERSE 14

I remain against or opposite to you because you hold more to that idea which is foreign to me, this false teaching which will cause you to fail, to decay; this idea has made a waste of the great strength which is in you. I am opposed to you—child of me though you be—while you inhale "the thing that is" (the breath of life) to no purpose, thus exerting yourself for naught and so committing idolatry, and constantly absorbing sorrow.

VERSE 15

And so do you align yourself with extinction—which is completely opposed to me, that is everlasting.

VERSE 16

Turn about or you will find confusion and "double talk" in all your doings (all your days, all your life).

VERSE 17

Use your ears, to hear what the spirit says to you at your center, in your inmost being. To that one (who uses his ears) will I give to absorb the "essence-of-*what*ness" (whatness, the entity of self). I will give a new dazzling keenness to guard and protect him and through that keenness will come a new nature known only to himself.

VERSE 18

That one, therefore, having sacrificed the old idea for this better one (Thyatira), hear this, from the very idea of Goodness itself, shining bright and firmly based:

VERSE 19

I know your works, your love, service, faith and patience, and again your works—these last works, being the *act*, are of more reward than the toilsome effort you first used.

VERSE 20

And still I have something against you also because you allow the false teaching of your human prophesying to inveigle my servants to commit idolatry and to absorb ideas of sorrow and trouble.

VERSE 21

Too long have you listened to this false teaching.

VERSE 22

Cohabit with this consciousness and worse trouble results—unless you deliberately cancel the false acceptance.

VERSE 23

All ideas of idolatry will die in the end and, deep within, you shall know that it is I—the Whole Spirit—that knows every thought of the mind, every emotion of the heart; and to every one will I give, in direct accord (or ratio) with his own action or toil.

VERSE 24

But to all of those who have not gone to the limits of opposition in their words, on them will I heap (add) no more trouble.

VERSE 25

Hold to the good till I come; or—hold on to the "false" until you recognize the Truth!

Chapter 2

VERSE 26

To those who express my actions through-out will I give power over all nations, to rule firmly,

VERSE 27

to completely crush out all that is contrary to Goodness.

VERSE 28

To these I will give *clear perception*.

VERSE 29

He that hath an ear, let him hear (See Verses 7, 11 and 17).

Chapter 3

VERSE 1

And to that driving force at the center, the originating center of those of you who, although you tremble, still have found your strength (Sardis), to you I say "hearken"; for I that speak in your heart am that complete fullness, unseen, but powerful for Good, powerful to arouse your own perfect and clear perception. *I AM within you*; because I am *within* you—I am in fact your very Self—I know your toil and your "effort-full" occupation. I know that your nature, in its present state of existence, longs for expressed action while yet seemingly impotent to act.

VERSE 2

Be on guard, alert and expectant, and *firmly* so, that you may inject vigor and ability into those failing acts, your dying resolutions. I do not find your efforts valiant enough in single-mindedness; there is too much vacillation in you. Your trembling is unnecessary.

VERSE 3

Recall the good which has come to you, fortify yourself and turn from your fears and your doubts! If you are not awake and alert to my presence I come but to leave, carrying away that which you think you have. I am not loud in announcing myself; even as a thief steals quietly upon you to rob you, even so I come quietly to bring you good. Expect me and listen carefully and constantly lest you fail to be aware!

VERSE 4

There are parts of your nature which, even at a time of trembling, do not break faith with the splendor of the high mood. These aspects shall accompany me in a dazzling sense of Self-awareness and shall be a force to strengthen your whole soul.

Chapter 3

VERSE 5

As you come up over and out of your weakness you shall be enveloped in a dazzling sense of joy. I will erase your present trembling nature out of your consciousness and thus announce the new awareness as the very author of Being in you, which Realization will proclaim the new state as a messenger to the world.

VERSE 6

Attune your ear and listen.

VERSE 7

And to those whose deep centers hold a love of mankind warm within (Philadelphia) declare: that in that deep center of love is the wholeness of love, is the wholeness of the world, is the established stability, is the very instrument which can open up more love. Whatever is done in the nature of True Love is not gainsaid by any man.

VERSE 8

I, the higher part of your nature, know all that your human self would do. Look intently and joyously, for I have provided the opportunity for you to turn about, to loosen your hold on preconceived ideas and ways; look, and observe the door—the way through which you may *"let down your bucket for drawing water"* (make inner contact with the indwelling Law of Good and draw forth a new consciousness). This way cannot be enclosed or held back from you by any man. There is nothing to restrict you, no one to restrain you or prohibit you by a word. Because you have exerted some firmness and followed, in part, my idea and have not entirely refused my nature, I give you this added chance to unite with me.

VERSE 9

Look closely and advise yourself that all of your untrue claims which *pretend* to be in accord with and searching for me, yet are not—these claims find themselves meeting with the opposition force and therefore expressing other than good in your life. Look joyously, for they will awake to their unhappy lot and will relax and join with your truer claims, because they will come to see that love of Truth—of the One Law of Good—is the thing which results in the full life.

VERSE 10

Because you have held to the idea of endurance, or continuing in love, I will keep you from the extreme testing of your human powers, which shall come to all who dwell in the world of form and matter.

VERSE 11

Understanding of ME comes quickly when you hold onto (and mull over) that much of understanding which you *do* have. No man can take away that dedication to truth which is *yours*.

VERSE 12

That one who attains self-mastery will become a support of (and exceedingly capable of) Good, and he will no longer find himself wavering. He will be engraved with the nature of Goodness and of that peacefulness which comes from the sense of the power of expansion. This new nature will be clearly stamped upon such a one.

VERSE 13

Listen well to all that the Breath of Life says within you!

VERSE 14

Finally, to that sense of Justice within you (Laodicia) declare: firmness and stability, fidelity and established security; these record sure evidence, from the basic principle, of the creation of Good.

VERSE 15

As I see you, from your works, you are not sure enough, you are not firmly *for* or definitely *against* ME—the Law of Good. I do not want you thus.

Chapter 3

VERSE 16

You cannot serve me in this manner for it is an untrue and an unsure expression.

VERSE 17

You *say* you are rich, with parrot-like affirmations. You *claim* to need nothing, but do not recognize that you make these claims with effort and with force. You are empty of Truth, full of pride and dissembling.

VERSE 18

Come to Me and recapture the purity of a burning flame, fiery hot in enthusiasm, that you may be abundantly supplied. Come and obtain the dazzling, glowing mood of joy that you may be wrapped in a mantle (a sense) of splendor, and that the sense of lack appear not. Exalt your outward appearance with humble content that you may see Truth.

VERSE 19

All those whom I love I correct and educate, I nurture and care for all whom I love, and they whom I love are *ALL*! Be filled with ardor, and a warm feeling of love that you may turn to Me—for

VERSE 20

look you: I am forever calling. It is the Spirit—the Self-Existent One in yourself—whispering in and with every breath: "Come unto ME, let down your bucket into the well of *living* water." I AM that very living water itself and will come in *on* your breath as an accumulation of answers to your call. We will mingle in the innermost depths of you.

VERSE 21

And in this mingling you will find yourself imbued with my power, and your understanding will expand as you continue to *breathe ME* (the breath of life). The human you, the divine you, and the over-all-originating-cause are one.

VERSE 22
Listen and BE that which you Eternally ARE.

Chapter 4

VERSE 1

Then I looked closely, with joy, and considering deeply within myself I began to draw from that inner depth a first sense of freedom which pointed to an expanded sense or state. As I searched for a meaning of this feeling, the disclosure vibrated through me as a conviction that the *Sound of God* was moving within me. It said: "Come, up and away from sense thought, and I will show you what will follow your recognition of ME."

VERSE 2

Instantly I lost all sense of the physical and at once a step in expansion was taken and power was present.

VERSE 3

That power was in accord with liberty and freedom, with salvation and prosperity, with healing; it was in definite relationship with the nature of the Father or Creative Source of all Being from which all children, as ideas, come. Besides this sense of the Creative Source there was also the feeling of receptive acceptance pouring forth with every step taken deeper into the expanded state; it was elating and strengthening, giving me the feeling of protection as from a strong tower.

VERSE 4

And about this feeling of power were surgings of plenty and appearances of abundance in dazzling form. I was protected from any faltering or unsureness, strengthened, even rededicated, as eager determination made the decision to surrender all doubt, and carve exactness of purpose.

Revelations on The Book of Revelation

VERSE 5

And from this step into greater expansion of consciousness came the shining happiness illuminating my mind, and the strong sound of "I Am the Self-Existent One" resounding through me and revealing the perfect radiating flame enclosing me—refining my desires into fragrant joy as I moved toward the Light. Each forward step was in the direction of the perfection of my consciousness as it approached the essence of all Good.

VERSE 6

Always before me was the opposite or alternative step, the "double outlet," the roar of the opposition reflecting as in a mirror the baldness of the old state and the crystal purity of the new. In the taking of this step could be found the strong aliveness of a new creation, the nearness of the change and the assurance that by abandoning all relations with the old, by praising "the new" as a secure aspect, it (the new) would be preserved as strongly as the old had been while all attention was devoted to it (the old).

VERSE 7

There were four strong emotions, each one alive and fresh. There was the emotion of violence and destruction which can keep your world in constant turmoil and chaos or which can be directed toward the destruction of the false or shadow things. Following *this* use of destruction there was the emotion of great joy, of exaltation at the idea of *re*-creation, of singing forth, "if able to bring forth an idea at all why not bring forth a desirable one?" This leads into the emotion of the availability of a vision which can *live*, can become existent as a *Man*-ifestation, the emotion which covers, in protection, this glorious idea till it comes alive, breathing Vitality in the assurance "our Lord has come."

VERSE 8

These four emotions churned about within me; there was brightness and cheer of a sort in all of them. They were visionary at their deepest center or inward part and constantly saying: The All

Mighty One, the Law of All Good, is perfect Wholeness, always was, IS NOW, and always is to be—*WHOLE*.

VERSE 9

Listening to this high praise and expression of reverence and value and power and adoration of the Eternal One, all the qualities that have been expressing in a limited way resign and make great ado over the envisioned state of perfection.

VERSE 10

They worship and say:

VERSE 11

The Law is indeed worthy of all praise and adoration, for IT is That which brings forth *ALL* things and brings them forth for the pure Joy of Creating.

Chapter 5

VERSE 1

And I perceived the strong freedom found in the High Self of Power. This High Self is the Life-Cause and declares: There is but One Mind, let us (the outer-appearing self and the inner, real Self) be set-at-one-again; ascend to your nearest part, The Center, and find perfection in the complete Truth of Being; the result will justify your acceptance of all this. This admonition or call from the Highest was sealed with seven seals [denoting intensity, opposition to your present state, and completeness].

VERSE 2

And I sensed a powerful messenger calling out the Divine Truth, making holy and whole with a shout of joy by a great vibration and asking, "Who is cheerful and strong enough to observe and to open his senses to the Cause, and so to dissolve the present state in order to be perfectly free to lift up the new state?"

VERSE 3

And no one who dwells in the factual realm of human reasoning can in any way sense this Cause of all Truth nor even perceive the deeper meaning.

VERSE 4

And I—the human, striving me—lamented the fact of human reasoning's inability to bring me out of my dilemma.

VERSE 5

And out of the abundance of knowing, from within myself, I heard: Do not lament; consider joyfully the pride in that which results from praise, that which is based in love, extending self through love, and from which all loving stems; this glowing, strong, praiseful, loving pride in your origin will be able to clarify all things.

Chapter 5

VERSE 6

And I looked joyfully, and wonder of wonders, in the center of that place of power and of the four emotions, in the very center of the Abundance of all Good, stood the strong male aspect—the Imagination—in its changed or uplifted form. The change showed the complete power and perfect perception which are the very Breath of Causative Essence already *in* the manifest form waiting to be used.

VERSE 7

And this strong aspect of Imagination took away that former aspect or the idea which had placed in power the manifestation of *itself*.

VERSE 8

And when the new idea had removed the imagining power of the old, the four emotions and the twenty-four abundances relinquished their former allegiance and bowed to the present Imagined Idea (Lamb), each of the elders (representing feelings of abundance) and all the emotions were singing and filled to overflowing with the sense of restful delight which is the whisper or breath of the Whole One.

VERSE 9

And they (the emotions and feelings of abundance in man) uttered or voiced a new desire, saying to the male aspect, or Imagination, in the midst of them: You are cheerful and deserving, and altogether suitable to go to this Originating Cause and to dissolve the stumbling-block of the appearance or present state. You are able to do this because you gave yourself wholly to the cause. Since it was you who set the seals, for protection, on the present (no-longer-desired) state, you are the one to breathe upon those seals and to dissolve them. It is *you*, the Imagination, which rescues us from the feeling of separation or aloneness and, severing our bondage to that feeling, takes us up to God or First Cause, making us again one with It (first cause) by the very act of *centering* us again in that eternal originating Truth. The silence of the center part of any one of us is the same as that of all classes of people, whatever their language or race or nation.

VERSE 10

And thus are we taken to the First Cause, thus we become one with It. Having entered or reached this Originating Cause we find, *surely*, the base or foundation of power, the sacred high realization of *This Point* as the beginning, the very commencement of all power. *This must be First*, thus do we find union—true union—and completeness.

VERSE 11

And I looked joyfully and felt the vibration of many messengers of hope round about the place of power, felt also the vibration of the emotions and all the qualities of abundance, unlimited in number.

VERSE 12

The assurance from this great vibration came: Strong and cheerfully deserving is the position of Imagination when coupled with the emotion which removes any sense of separation-from-the-originating-cause, sacrificing the old or undesired state and giving itself wholly to the new or desired state. The realization within you that *this is the thing to do* is indeed laudable and deserving of power and riches and wisdom and strength and honor and glory and blessing.

VERSE 13

And all created ideas in the state of expansion, and those already formed (even if depressed), and those trying to break forth, all expressed and vibrated blessing and honor and glory and power to that one who is conscious of his inner power and ability to unite Joyous Imagination to Receptivity for ever and ever.

Chapter 5

VERSE 14

And the emotions said: So be it! And the feelings of abundance gave themselves over, wholly, to the Eternal Originating Cause which never ceases to make all things new.

Chapter 6

VERSE 1

And I—the unfolding human side of me—began to be aware of greater depths: I discerned that the vision of unfoldment, the Lamb, the strong male aspect of unlimited Imagination, freed one's binding sense of limitation. I listened attentively and intently. I yielded to the *inner breath* and a great Tone, as a Voice, sounded in me and one of the four emotions said: "Come and see"—*BE*—and care for or cherish your Visions!

VERSE 2

And I considered further and discerned, looking intently and with joy, a dazzling lightness of joy; and I sensed that, maintaining and riding with joy, joyous and joyful things would be produced and brought forth, in the very nature of things. The joyous rider was encircled with protection and he went forth to victory, overcoming all that did not yield to joy.

VERSE 3

(Same as Verse 1.)

VERSE 4

And there was another side to this joy: it was red, fire-like, boiling with trouble, joying in the foul things, a self-contained hurricane which could make an end to its own joy. To this aspect is given the capacity to destroy the union of complete oneness between any expression and its source, allowing the separated expressions or manifested appearances to keep the mind in suspense and so destroy each other. Into the hand of this false one was put the weapon of destruction—the shoot or outgrowth of its own kind, loosed upon itself—the terrible sword of separation.

Chapter 6

VERSE 5

(Same as Verses 1 and 3): And I looked intently and was joyed to see, riding the Idea of Joy, one who, though mourning, was seeking in the obscurity for a poise, a sense of balance betwixt joying-in-trouble-and-bringing-destruction and joying-in-sheer-joy, which was its own protection. How can these be coupled?

VERSE 6

Vibrating deep in the center of the four emotions I discerned a message, saying: Stretch yourself, purge the unwanted, purify yourself and grow, increase beyond the value of a penny, intensify your thinking and distinguish between the trouble and the light, decide not to destroy, overthrow or hinder the light nor to crush the effervescing glow of joy.

VERSE 7

(Same as Verses 1, 3, and first part of 5.)

VERSE 8

And I looked again with intentness, and the horse—the joyful emotion—was pale, as from shame or fright, because its rider was considering "outward appearance" which always leads to a sense of separation (death). [The hell which follows is that, even when the "outward appearance" is a joyous one, if the constant attention is allowed to dwell on or remain with the appearance, forgetting the source, then calamity, cessation, complete reversal of joy must follow. Capacity is given to this limiting condition to send away joy and even the craving for joy, thus the emotions become dulled and manifestation becomes limited and brought to near extinction.]

VERSE 9

And as I continued to look and become aware of greater depths I discerned, beneath the breath of shame at separation, a change—a transmuting of that shame to the Breath of Spirit; for It, the Breath of Spirit, cannot die. It is but sealed up for protection until the Idea of Good is restored and through use again expressed,

23

Revelations on The Book of Revelation

VERSE 10

and the urge cries out within man: How long before the Whole, True Law will extend and stretch itself and vindicate our confidence in all manifest forms?

VERSE 11

And shining splendor and excellence were given to them all and they were told to pause and to reverse themselves, delaying in order to allow an opportunity to all who had associated with them to be consecrated and thus caused to be perfected and completed. [All those who felt separated and continued to consort with the Idea of Death and Hell would be destroyed.]

VERSE 12

And I, the unfolding, human side of me, continued to look; and I discerned a great vibration and I grew afraid, for brilliance and light and happiness became darkened as when in sorrow and separation, and all youthful illumination and attractiveness became silent and empty.

VERSE 13

And suddenly the visions of expansion began to come to expression; and they were as premature children, arriving too soon to be completely strong, causing false imaginings (though capable of giving quite the opposite).

VERSE 14

And the idea of expansion revealed the understanding that comes from communion with God when that communion is complete and touches the Inner True Self. Out of this comes true expiation of sin, for there is a cessation of all questioning, lifting one to a perfect state of relaxation, letting the unsearchable rest in Mind.

VERSE 15

And the ability to do, and the capability of discernment, and the freedom of experience, and the eminence of determination, and the valiant builders—all these came together to lie in wait till light should break, to dream how they might exalt themselves.

VERSE 16

And they said: Exalting and dreaming can overwhelm that which strives for continued appearance in the place of power,

VERSE 17

for the great breaking forth of a New Imagining comes quickly on the heels of a desire to change, and no undesired state or condition can continue to exist.

Chapter 7

VERSE 1

And after dreaming and exalting the True Self, came the breaking forth of fresh creative power, delineating success in new manifestation, but retaining the basic power of comprehension (of the Creative Breath) which brings manifestation, and pointing out that we should not bind ourselves again by imaging duality—for what we image is made FIRM!

VERSE 2

And I was conscious of another driving message exalting me with intensity, reversing the former evil of duality, and holding up a new definite goal, attesting to the preserved secret of the breathing vitality of the State of Goodness. This intense urge vibrated within me; its power *could* lay the foundation for further duality, and yet the force of it lifted me to cry:

VERSE 3

Do not break in pieces the manifest form to make manifestation good for nothing! Destroy *nothing*, neither of duality nor of firmness, until we have secured the idea of the compelling power of Goodness and stamped it deep and clear in the very breathing nature of all persons.

VERSE 4

And I pondered the value of separation which is preserved in the secret of opposition. There is a kind of opposition which, as a mother, is able to measure or impel the generation of new abundance, producing the completeness of God-like, powerful strength.

Chapter 7

VERSE 5

Praise and Thanksgiving, the most binding and solid form of worship, are substances which sprout into or become the very support of life. This Truth is closed up and stamped for secure preservation, to be learned as Two—hence duality and trouble, or as Ten, the perfection of One, on into infinity. There is also support to be found in vision, support to build upon in like manner, as separation *or* Unity. Again this producing may be crowded and seem fearsome, as perhaps bringing attack and dissension; or the crowd may be seen as a fortunate richness.

VERSE 6

Prosperity and happiness are linked with honesty and straightforwardness, and this Truth is also attested to as solid and sure when inculcated into the offshoot of the mind. More is preserved in this great accumulation of digits, to wit: that *Breathing aright* produces a *refreshing expansion*. [This can be seen as merely lung expansion or as breathing greatness into living!] In this hidden message is also the power to forget; this can be a calamity or a blessing, according to what is forgotten and why!

VERSE 7

Sealed in the mystery of ten and two is the part that hearing plays, for to hear with the two physical ears is to hear confusion, but to hear with the One ear of perceptive discernment is to hear with Understanding. It is also necessary to be watchful about that to which you become *attached*—it can cause mourning or serve as an ornament to bring joy. There are many rewards and benefits to be found in this mystery sealed within yourself, to be lifted out by yourself.

VERSE 8

Again, sealed in this mystery of ten and two, is the idea of *abiding or dwelling* with or in a state bringing an *increase of or addition to* that condition or dwelling place. The very act of continuing in that state being in itself *firm and strong* as the *right hand*, symbol of active manifestation of an idea cradled in passive acceptance.

VERSE 9

Then I looked joyfully and wonder of wonders, countless people on every hand beyond enumeration or computation, of all races and tribes and languages, all stood before the idea of the Power of Imagination. The emotion engendered in them at the idea of this unlimited power enveloped them in dazzling splendor and they stood erect claiming the power offered to them.

VERSE 10

And the vibration was strong; the Power of Goodness has placed your deliverance in you as the center of Power, as Imagination, as the ability to raise the Consciousness and realize *it* to be the only Ruler.

VERSE 11

And all the aspects of possible expression (or being), astonished, but drawing near to worship, were silent, waiting and friendly, enveloped in light, seeking to commune with the idea of power, encircled with the idea of abundance and also with the engendering emotions. This combination caused them to draw nearer and acknowledge all Good,

VERSE 12

Saying: It is so. Universal Goodness is the right, the happy, the straight way, filled with dignity, understanding, cheerfulness, value, virtue, valor, strength, wholeness. SO IT IS.

VERSE 13

Out of the abundance came the answer: Would to God the self, the gallant thing of splendor (veiled as yet) would consider and know itself: know that it is out of the Self-Same Source or Cause of all things! When will you see this?

VERSE 14

And I said unto him: Only that which is supreme in authority can answer. And he said: This thing (implying you, or the prostrate ones) this thing is the *Only Self*. This self came forth out of trouble, out of a tight place; that which rivals it or is opposed to the True Self came forth from cohabitation with the opposing thought, but having seen the light has conquered the covering, the obstruction, and come forth a dazzling, shining thing—shining in the confidence of the life-giving power of its own God-given Imagination.

VERSE 15

And this union is the cause of all things. Draw near this place of power within yourself where Goodness dwells and worship this Higher Self constantly in the sacred withinness, and as it (the human self) dwells there marry or unite with IT in that center place of closeness and be the BRIDE OF GOD.

VERSE 16

This True Self will keep the human self from craving or toiling and from suffering; the inflaming blaze of anger shall no longer trouble the human self.

VERSE 17

For the wonder of Vital Imagination which is in the heart-center, the powerful place of feeling, shall consume all lesser suggestions and shall transport them to the active, primary source of overwhelming refreshment. The realization of True Goodness erases all that is contrary to Goodness, leaving the human self elevated above the flood of trouble, riding the crest of the revelation of its own True Self. Lamentation and weeping cannot exist where a true understanding of *all Good* is.

Chapter 8

VERSE 1

And when this great Imaginative Power *in me* became aware of the ultimate perfection—preserved, yet available—it was astonished and I was filled with the quiet of trustful waiting. I was refreshed as I perceived the unlimited opportunity in my own midst or center and I considered the fulfillment of deliverance from bondage.

VERSE 2

And I perceived the perfect messengers abiding in Goodness and arranging powerful vibrations and shining light.

VERSE 3

And another messenger came, eager to surrender all personal feeling for the sake of exactness in his announcement; he stood boldly out to speak and to manifest cheerfully the divine assurance of Goodness. I felt a great lifting and easing of the heart and I yielded to the invitation to draw near and converse with my Real Self in the sacred place where we are WHOLE, and to feel my breath, as I sacrifice it or let go, move toward and mingle with that "other" which is my SELF. All of this promises POWER of the *right* kind.

VERSE 4

And so the anger, the heaviness and the personal pride (enclosed at the center of my heart or feeling nature) rushed forth, sacrificed, as I breathed and made a motion toward greater understanding, as I called upon the consecrated and more perfect state of mind—drawn near by ascending in consciousness—trusting, praising, drawing ever nearer the essence of pure Goodness, and feeling the message of power thrill through me.

Chapter 8

VERSE 5

And the messenger accepted the destruction of the anger and heaviness, and replaced it with the burning flame of joyous sacrifice, throwing out all that stood in opposition to the new sense of wholeness. This caused great confusion and uproar and trembling. Through it the great Tone or Vibration of the Self-Existent One flashed as an illumination of clarity and happiness.

VERSE 6

And all the messengers or proclamations of the perfect reverberation set in order the vitality of the self-chosen, wholesome discipline, which would lead to the Wholeness of Integrity and generate Truth.

VERSE 7

And the unity of the command was as a shout of Triumph joining together in deep understanding the calm and cheerful (but burningly intense) desire to give security and to dissolve the sense of separation, thus destroying the duality implicit in a sense of opposition. An intense amount of strength was refined in the process and new prosperity was turned into fragrant joy.

VERSE 8

And the shout of Triumph was doubled and all sense of sin was consumed and the feeling of expiation flamed with intensity, ejecting the last remnant of "separateness" with a roar, intensifying the destruction of shame, so that it perished altogether.

VERSE 9

And all that lived in a sense of disgrace was utterly destroyed. That intense feeling of separateness which had seemed a fixture perished.

VERSE 10

Again the shout of Triumph intensified, and an increase of light and a perception of the ability to expand overwhelmed me, radiating as a glow, intensely shining; and it was accepted and used as belonging to the idea of prosperity, accepted also as the true Source of Consciousness.

VERSE 11

At first this new perception disclosed bitterness and calamity, and a deep portion of my consciousness grew discontented, and many manifestations ceased because of this inner rebellion.

VERSE 12

Once more there was a shout of Triumph, this time with a weaker vibration, and the sense of happiness was somewhat oppressed, as was the understanding and the vision; therefore as the intensity of these Three was concealed, even obscured, my earnestness and diligent searching no longer rejoiced but closed up within me.

VERSE 13

And I looked intently and heard a word expressed in extremity as if being withdrawn from, even bisecting my heart. The vibration of the word I heard expressed a great longing, a weakness and a fear. I trembled, for the opposition seemed so strong, and it seemed that the vibrations yet to come could limit me.

Chapter 9

VERSE 1

And a fifth messenger spoke, and a vision spread before me, expanding into the form of a promise to open the profound mystery.

VERSE 2

Observing the mystery there was felt, at first, a sense of heaviness because of the very profundity of it all. The anger of subjugation enveloped me, I felt violated, subdued and disregarded, and my illumined happiness and power—my very perception—was again obscured; for power misused becomes anger and fear and hides better judgment.

VERSE 3

And out of anger came an increase in the form of the undesirable things, which same do have the capacity to bring forth abundance; even as a scourge, having temporary strength, can force its likeness into abundant expression.

VERSE 4

And I heard a decree that the scourge should not crush or destroy the "sprouting ability" or the "power-of-bringing-forth-into-form," nor should it crush any other new and firm states; for only such inclinations as have in them nothing of the "secret nature" of Goodness *can* be destroyed.

VERSE 5

And this force of anger was not permitted to destroy utterly, but only to torture for a time. This infliction was as the vexation of any scourge, which limits a person or condition *until new understanding liberates it*, to permit advancement.

VERSE 6

In the midst of the scourging even the courageous *consider* destruction, to end their despair; actually there is no end—they can come forth from despair. Although they long to cease trying, a "doing-nothing" state will always elude them.

VERSE 7

The perversion and these undesired appearances was such that they resembled joyous objects arranged as things of value, but were arrayed (encamped) to bring hardship. These false things were "shaky," uncertain and unsure; eager determination hid behind the appearance, and courage of a sort also was there.

VERSE 8

Being false, they suggested separation, and caused abandonment of what, at one time, had been professed, thus bringing forth the two-edged wish (or thought-with-the-double-meaning) which brings about destruction.

VERSE 9

And these undesired appearances sparkled richly as though they could transport with love, and they purported to set me free. They had about them a fearfulness which frightened me, but showed themselves without blemish at the center whence they raised themselves. I saw the duality (the two possibilities) run together, fitting with integrity into a perfect whole, so vast and so surely complete that the two skipped for joy as they flowed together. They were renewed, restored to new life, revived and saved; for however separated the two possibilities may seem, nonetheless AT THE CENTER is that God (Good-saving) essence which if touched—even inadvertently—will cause a rapid coming together of the two seeming opposites. Always the weak or doubtful, even if antagonistic, is absorbed into and raised up by the Good—the complete Wholeness—and ends by worshipping perfection.

Chapter 9

VERSE 10

Thus they (those undesired appearances) could cut off or curtail me in the manner of a scourge, or they could wound in order to separate me from the sense of poison and point out *in the wounding* the center of divine impulse to which I could give myself wholly. The capacity or strength of these undesired appearances could have charge of affliction and indicate harm or hinder development, thus injuring; OR, as they carved or fashioned with friendly intent, *could* hurt in order to strengthen and cure, to set free and extend experience, to increase discernment and right choice for the purpose of rebuilding, repairing and renewing.

VERSE 11

Ruling over these appearances was a negative force, which is the aspect of destruction, whose nature is to assume *similarity or opposition*. When this ruler expresses similarity to the undesirable it is a destroying aspect, in that it makes one seem to lose oneself. When, however, this ruler effervesces in active opposition to the undesirable, the destruction is then in reverse, destroying that which is *un*desirable.

VERSE 12

Greatly desiring, the Real Self projects or comes forth from within. This desire is unsearchable and past finding out, but look joyfully—it beats upon the consciousness regularly, in constant repetition, with double strength, with increased yearning.

VERSE 13

And a cheerful messenger, rejoicing in the promise of abundance which would follow the practice of self-discipline and self-control (the beginning of integrity) sang his message which echoed through my ears. I consented to search further for the vital power of secret surrender which breathes through me as I praise and move toward absolute Goodness.

VERSE 14

And the message was full of bright happiness and suggested to those who felt bound that they release their inner vibration (pent up breath) in order to dissolve the sense of sin. For this dissolving alone can expiate the feeling of separation which is the real sin—this is the center of strength within each one awaiting recognition and release.

VERSE 15

And the vitality of the messages dissolves the captive's bands when the captive has arranged and set in order his sense of values, when he has inspected with respect and considered the possibility of renewing and rebuilding with a desire to transmute the old, to abolish the old limitations and to intensify the new heritage.

VERSE 16

And the resources of valor and strength and wealth were myriad; and I understood their valuation.

VERSE 17

After this manner I moved toward comprehension and I regarded with pleasure and discernment the revelation of joy. The vitality of the breath itself caused a feeling of ascendancy, of enduring life, a realization of the very entity of freedom to be found in turning to the heart or center of Self. It is necessary to *think toward* the inner value in order to discover the "feel" of divinity. The promise of Joy was as violent as the former sense of violence and pride. Proceeding forth from this new inner Joy was a disciplined Self which brought forth wisdom and happiness as a fountain of water glowing and luminous at the center, feeble as yet, but approaching the divine.

VERSE 18

Through this intensity some have their courage destroyed by the very bonds of consuming thought and anger which flow from their own condemnation. It is self-destruction emanating from their own center, based on their own baffled doubts. A third of mankind does destroy itself through inner bitterness and loss of unity with the divine.

VERSE 19

They do so because within themselves they have a strength and capacity to discipline themselves and speak in accordance with Almighty God OR to curtail themselves through fear. If the latter, they exist in vexation and affliction by reason of shriveling up inside till they cannot see clearly or *straight*. They whisper a magic spell of harm upon themselves and destroy their own power and so hinder their progress.

VERSE 20

Those who were not destroyed or curtailed by a sense of defeat still did not turn about to the grasping of the means of power which is ever near and which would keep them from worry and anger over the appearance of opposition. Instead, they gave homage to the adversity, felt terror, exerted themselves for naught at sight of glittering promise, and desired the *ornaments* of power, even though they were fetters and very weighty and firmly fastened. This terror blinded their vision, dulled their understanding and limited their ability to travel or to truly live.

VERSE 21

Thus dulled, they could not escape the spell of destruction which covered them and caused them to look *OUT* upon things rather than to remain centered and poised in the Self; thus were they seemingly carried away from that Self.

Chapter 10

VERSE 1

And I became aware of another messenger, a powerful one, which although it was enveloped in secrecy, I discerned because it was strong and firm. It came as a teacher to instill humility—not a supine state but a willingness to consider and weigh all sides and to listen to the inner voice which speaks a language of illumination and happiness. To understand this will always give dependable support, for it is of the within, of the Spirit itself.

VERSE 2

This messenger held the means of power, the very cause of "releasing-for-the-purpose-of-beginning-again." He established freedom and justice in the midst of the dual appearance, determining which of the two states or conditions was true, and allowing *it* to remain, consecrating this right one of the two as the one which was the most just and the nearest to the state of wholeness, leaving behind in abasement the obstinate or "hard" state which had tried to dominate by opposition and to prostrate by binding.

VERSE 3

Then the messenger proclaimed in a clear and cheerful tone, but withal a majestically vehement and strong one, proclaimed the Self-Existent One as an inner strong vibration to be sought for with perceptive awareness. Unrecognized for its powerful goodness this inner vibration can crush with the violence of its force, agitating and troubling the senses, perplexing the mind, confounding and confusing in great insurrection. Recognized, this commotion can be turned into meditative study and emit forgiveness and send forth the clear shout or sound of joy or freedom—the perfect sound—announcing clearly that intelligent understanding of this true Self, the Self-Existent One, speaks of great Good immanent.

Chapter 10

VERSE 4

And when this perfect realization had stood boldly forth predicting or explaining this great truth I was hampered from all sides, but determined to seek for learning. Desiring to undertake greater search I anticipated persuasion, and was willing to yield to the authority of that vibration which was shaking me from the very depths of my being. I gave good heed and sensed the order to oppose my known or mortal self, and the personal lusts of *sheer* sensual pleasure in order to yield to the Divine Self also present within me— the perfect vibration of the Self-Existent One.

VERSE 5

And the messenger of whom I was aware continued to hold his peace, resisting the double appearance and the approach of opposition; he began to rouse from his inactivity and to raise himself, to draw upon his inner power of expansion;

VERSE 6

he rebelled at the power of opposition and of duality, desiring rather to be complete; he expiated all sense of separation from the active breathing reality of eternity which constantly causes expression; and I determined never again to be driven off the course which leads to competence and abundance.

VERSE 7

When that perfect messenger shall commence to search out integrity and real sincerity, to discipline the mind as well as the body, he will generate the preparation for the secret of Goodness to be revealed, even as this High Goodness has already announced to his children, through the inspired ones. To them, HE, the Self Cause or Creator, has agreed in a binding compact to rain (to fall in drops of constant and continued abundance) through mental desires. [Could also be to *reign*.] Accept these desires as from the High-Self, arise and sing about them, and they shall be completed, and *you made complete*.

VERSE 8

And the great Vibration of disclosure was divinely intimate. It sounded through me and persuaded me to consent to listen further that I might expand in intelligence; it communed with me; it revealed the Divine Expression and affirmed a thought which could lead me on to release and transcendence. This was the thought which sang through me: Lift the ineffective cause which you have been espousing; eschew the faint-hearted word; be observant to the approach of power coming with the messenger who is to arouse you to your existence—above duality. This true existence is to be found in and through your motion toward your own center of balance, that center which at first glance seems to oppose your way of life; in reality you may rest in that center as it is the firm opposition to weakness.

VERSE 9

And so I approached the messenger and said: Make known to me the ineffectiveness of a separated cause. And he said: Continuing to feel separated from the Creative Cause of all Life is to plunder your own possessions, to destroy the progress toward your perfection, to prostitute your experiences which are given you to overcome, to accept and use as an inheritance (not to oppose or resist). Profane your experiences and you pervert them to hollow discontent, even though you speak of them as desirable and agreeable sweetness.

VERSE 10

And yet I continued in my perversion and self-destruction, selecting and choosing of my own free will to destroy my faith and shun the truth. There was pleasure and heady sweetness in many things, but soon was manifest a dissolution in all about me and violent rebellion surged up in me.

VERSE 11

And the messenger responded to my defiance, saying: You must change your mental desire and sing with inspiration: gain a new

Chapter 10

vision and—perceiving it—remain in contemplation of that new vision until you feel lifted from despair and in and of yourself accept the advance, the inspired message, and shout it to all peoples, whatever their language or race or nation.

Chapter 11

VERSE 1

And a great light shone upon me, ready to aid me in procuring redemption, that I might correct my error and be able to re-create and support myself. And the messenger confirmed the promise of the light and offered to stand near, ready to enhance my power of endurance and to arrange the substitution of the Divine Expression for the seeming opposite, thus bringing about a moral recovery which would lead me to my goal or establish my purpose. This awakened me spiritually so that I was able to estimate my ability and to extend my capacity and vitality as a breathing, creating self, either to continue in worry and pain or to carve out glory and dignity by reverencing Goodness.

VERSE 2

But the consciousness which is the center of all capacity must be allowed to remain, reserving it to aid in the completion of that good-omened promise and not limiting or shaking it. For consciousness is ordained for *usage*, to use for the purpose of mounting, of increasing and of growing in glorious majesty. Should this consciousness be limited, the pure, chaste revelation of wholeness would be split open, divided, so as to crush, rejecting with disdain the new hope and reverting to the duality of the old.

VERSE 3

And the messenger said: Mastery, valor and endurance, the ability to persevere and give life, respond in two ways: falsely to rob—which is untrue testimony with regard to God; uprightly to restore—which is to understand, to note carefully, to hear or perceive intelligently—this is inspiration. When you associate with inspiration, myriad countless units of growth—as a producing mother—intensify the earnest seeking and stretch out in great expansion, extending your stature.

VERSE 4

And the same double-edged or dual fruitfulness is rich and firm in its strength and substantiation, whether it be *for* or *against* Goodness.

VERSE 5

And if any breathing creature confuse or hinder the inspiration toward Goodness, brilliant light leaps forth to enlighten, to shine clearly and draw together the issue, repeating the same speech or admonition: that the inspiration of Goodness is to be desired earnestly, overcoming the confusion or opposition which leads to continued trouble and hatred. Destruction always follows confusion when the attention speaks the word of confusion as a desired mode of action.

VERSE 6

These confusions are able to cramp expansion and unfoldment, restricting the flow of joyous abundance which mental desires are intended to draw forth. They are able to influence these desires, transferring them to failure, destroying them by force of opposition into calamity and defeat, thus delaying the expression of Goodness.

VERSE 7

Finally the extreme confusion ceases to confuse and begins to prepare the self for restoration. Alive and refreshed, the self arises from the infernal depths which seemed so negative, examines the experience and realizes the profound lesson gained. This realization chooses to admit the indisputable strength which results from recognizing negation and weak submission but crossing over to firmness and control of the outer self.

VERSE 8

Idolatrous images with their flabby and foolish uselessness, the fears and weaknesses which prey on the mind and on the heart—*all these* are made of the same substance as are the sound, whole images of Good. Chasing the untrue, causes a sense of separation from Goodness, twisting the thought from mental joy, it invites the scorching limitation of a hostile opposition. But, opposition need not oppose, in any active or antagonistic sense—opposition is but another point of view. The Law proclaims the wisdom of "crossing-over," or viewing all sides, exploring all possibilities easily, relaxedly, in order to draw forth the Good which is ever-present at all times.

VERSE 9

All this disturbance has a relationship to speech and usage, which all too often render impotent vital substance that is intended for powerful good. Earnest, intense and diligent search should be centered in the good, indifferent to pain or hardship, pressing on toward again expressing soundness and wholeness, putting confusion itself to confusion, finding repose to lean upon and erasing the wound or hurt. This result makes atonement, indeed, cancelling or destroying the hurt, freeing entirely the remembrance and carving a new prayer in the heart.

VERSE 10

Standing firm and fast on this new prayer state, intensifying the joyous feeling, all "opposites" become counterparts and complements, revealing the God-ward way of crossing over from one state to another, revealing that separation is external only—in reality all are one for ALL IS ONE. Illumination and complete assurance or conviction of this gladdens the heart and makes known the sound, the beautiful and the good. Praise almost overwhelms one, divorcing past fears and fully releasing the allotted share of divine gratitude and joy. This illumination brings its own causal agreement as a touch-stone shiningly inspired and foretelling that one day opposition will be recognized as but two sides of the *same* thing.

Chapter 11

VERSE 11

Furthermore, closely accompanying this intense search for illumination, the breath of life balanced and centered within as the very present existence of the soul, became consciously active and revealed itself as the very mode or means of all vitality, ever at hand and ready to aid in any way to prove itself and to provide assistance in establishing the Self. This victorious understanding increased the abiding reverence and trust and made it clear that faithlessness resulted in a fright which eventuated in a sense of separation and a driving of one's self off the course, thus bringing about great depression.

VERSE 12

Increased abundance of the new ideas vibrated through me, and refuted the false sense of separation and exalted my feelings so that I was enveloped in refreshment, and all the hateful hostility and affliction of trouble was as if it had never been.

VERSE 13

Inspecting this same new feeling, considering it with joy, a mighty vibration shook me and again my consciousness rocked with the horror of possible separation from this great good, this good for which I longed with all my heart. Weakness depressed me (or perhaps it was depression which weakened me) and I gave myself wholly to the vibration for protection. Suddenly I experienced courage and power as a strong, fortifying help pouring in to refill my senses, teaching me anew. Discouragement again left me and I turned back to my original starting place, giving myself over to perseverance in finding the light (understanding), giving praise and worship and exulting in the surge of joy.

VERSE 14

The double melancholy having been turned back, I looked intently and an intense desire swiftly appeared.

VERSE 15

And the messenger of perfection proclaimed, with increased vibration: The foundation of all power, for eternity, is the principle of the Law and of its Realization. This Realization of the Law is basic and brings about completeness and perfect union everlastingly, IT is the WHOLENESS or Holy One.

VERSE 16

And the surgings of plenty and appearances of abundance dwelling in Goodness entered upon a reversed course and breathed forth healing power,

VERSE 17

uttering the Divine Expression: "None of these outer things move or change me" for all praise and power are vested in the Mighty Law of Good which hath existed from all time and will be unto all time, as the One Cause ascribing and bringing forth infinite capacity for sustaining complete Wholeness and perfection.

VERSE 18

The habits of people made them stretch out for the good they desired, avidly, passionately clutching for it; foolishly they let the false habits rule, expecting compensation as their right. Habits are intended to serve, to be consecrated and to reverence the nature of perfect Goodness; when they forget their place and wander away they fail in their purpose and are entirely useless, causing destruction through antagonism.

VERSE 19

The infinite capacity for good is to be observed through inner expansion. Dreaming deeply on this infinite capacity for good one may gather the enlightenment to experience or to receive the high purpose which will flow through one, as through a channel; illumination and happiness, a vibration of power, all these surge through mightily as a salutation from on high, SAYING:

Chapter 11

BE WELL
BE GLAD
GOD SPEED

Chapter 12

VERSE 1

Increasing ability and power were revealed through this vision of Goodness, an ability which could cause great happiness to be expressed, albeit this same power was concealed from casual examination. With increased understanding, however, one chooses justice and attains victory, and is thereby protected and inspired to learn more, to perceive with greater clarity the inner truths which, though concealed for preservation, are awaiting discovery and are ready to reveal magnificent and unlimited power.

VERSE 2

This Causal Power, when *un*recognized, is as a tyrant. Misdirected, it tires, grieves and distresses, bringing forth undesirable states and causing wearing effort to accompany all acts. On the other hand as soon as the marvelous potential of this Creative Force is recognized and fully realized it becomes at once the Loving Master and the Servant (SERVER) who joys to fulfill in complete response all expressed hope, forgiving the twisted request, rescuing the former self and restoring the True Self.

VERSE 3

In expansion toward Goodness increasing ability and power are constantly revealed. The *glory* of this power is its limitlessness, the *fear* of it is that it works both ways. Great knowledge, disunited from Truth and Goodness, becomes a frightful monster which destroys and weakens. Recognition of Goodness as the sacred and principal thing which is full of power to make or to create *ITSELF* (i.e. *all* Goodness), this recognition is our protection and our consecration.

Chapter 12

VERSE 4

The feeling of being "cut-off" (intense separation) from the Father (or Goodness itself) gives just as great and intense a feeling of separation as the opposite state gives of unity. Cut off from the ability to cause good is the greatest destruction possible, and is even as a monster looming up in opposition and confirming alone-ness. Be prepared for this dual possibility, be not afraid of the undesirable but be steadfast in considering the desirable. Be diligent in expectation of only good, strengthen your belief, and desire earnestly to live true to the highest idea you can bring forth, and you will beget or produce a Savior.

VERSE 5

When this good news—or this promise—bursts upon your consciousness you will know that you are "He That Hath IT," that is, you are one with the inner ability to produce (from or out of your own self) your own Savior or Saving Power, are one with the quality of perfect service which rules *with* LOVE and *for* GOOD, irrespective of former beliefs. This rule bears within it its own form of correction and is the very support of Life, for it is the Substance of Law itself, assuring the expression, in form, of a replica of any inward unformed thought. It is vital to realize the difference between FEAR and REVERE, for the unformed thought must express in form like unto its invisible self. Fear or shun that unformed thought which is *un*kind or centered in the personal self, revere or welcome that unformed thought which is *kind*—which is the SELF ITSELF. There is no redress from the law of "like begetting like." Then let your child—your idea—be captured by Goodness and united to its power.

VERSE 6

Obscuring or shunning this law leads to sterility of ideas, at least for a time, until at last the unimportance of material things is recognized and there dawns the realization of the great value of spiritual unfoldment as the greatest need of existence. Convinced of this, Goodness arranges opportunities and conditions which lead to true liberty and increase the abundance of all things, thus teaching the right or true meaning of duality which is, in a measure, the mother or bringer-forth of all conditions.

VERSE 7

Duality *misunderstood* causes the expansion of Goodness to be contracted. Understood, however, duality is revealed as interesting and needful. The aspects of Goodness, wherever found, move toward perfect expression and dissolve or absorb any appearance of antagonism, for moving God-ward *nothing* can be evil, and any appearance which seems momentarily so must be encompassed and dissipated.

VERSE 8

No appearance of "less-than-good" is of truth and therefore can never prevail or overpower, beyond a limited space of time.

VERSE 9

So no matter how severe or vast the monstrous appearance, it is ejected and sent away. For the fear which did appeal to or summon the thoughts—as a God, even though a false one—shows itself to be an opponent, an adversary to the truth, enrapturing the senses as it deludes them all at least for the moment. None-the-less this monstrous and opposing force *is* thrown out of its role of antagonistic opponent and all aspects which are at variance to the perfect truth are also sent away or rejected.

VERSE 10

And I understood the strength and vehemence of the vibration affirming the expansion of health, declaring the victorious deliverance and liberty which are possible in unlimited abundance as the very foundation of all power which lies in pure Goodness and perfect understanding. For the false use of that which appears to be an affinity—or desirable state—is sloughed off in the very act of seeking with sincerity to know Goodness, and in recognizing it even when it is twisted into a seeming ill.

Chapter 12

VERSE 11

And the recognition of this truth again prevailed and dissolved the opposition at the very center of its life-force, dissolved it through right use of the Imagination, through reversal of false thought, and through announcing the Divine Idea of restoring the precept of True Principle. Thus was restored the determination to exist as intended, free and sure, and to destroy anything less than Pure Goodness.

VERSE 12

Therefore be exceedingly glad in your ability to expand and to stand firm in the expansion of your choice! Have no wish for the false or antagonistic state of mind, that dual state which causes indecision, for this state of indecision is of itself a god, one which depresses and subdues, which frustrates and excites the mind. Recognizing its own transience it seeks to take every opportunity to pull down.

VERSE 13

And when the monstrous condition was discerned and discarded as opposing the desired state, it "ran after" that causative idea which continues to put up with or endure vacillation.

VERSE 14

And the causative power arose again to its own highest place, breathing with an increasing sense of uplift as it again approached that place of "forking"—of choice. It desired to maintain greater firmness as it received its new opportunity—trust from the center of being which whispered: "to learn by experience is an expression of Divinity."

VERSE 15

And fear spoke, attempting to influence again the causative impulse and divide its allegiance, causing retreat and a return to captivity by increasing dissension and keeping the suspenseful state alive.

VERSE 16

But fear of opposition, understood, could deliver the causative force from its indecision, thus it might absorb the prosperity and happiness which fear—in the form of a monster—had thrown away.

VERSE 17

Fear raged at the causative power, trying to provoke or crack it, undertaking to sow lack and destitution. But, all evidence pointed to the failure of fear, as the Recorder of Good came forth to guard and to protect, testifying that the highest realization of the reality of a present power-of-Good (an *every*where present, an *omni*present power-of-Good) always would prevail in the long run.

Chapter 13

VERSE 1

For the power of Good is always at hand, ready to rise within *s*elf and to raise Self, to draw together these two (the human, limited self and the Divine, Limitless Self) which continue to endure as one, rising above the possibility of perverting the close association into duality. I discerned the strong, vital conclusion ascending to or from its own origin by the way of duality, and bringing to pass understanding of existence sufficient to furnish full and sacred completeness—the veritable principle of expressing Self through rays of power. These rays of power encircle the *s*elf for protection, dedicating it to the ultimate triumph of its own inherent nature of wise authority. When scorned or neglected this nature acts as a curse, but reversing the scorn to awareness of the deeper nature, the little *s*elf becomes betrothed to the Real Self, surrenders itself and is blessed by uniting with its real nature.

VERSE 2

This vital, strong aliveness which I discerned resembled pure water in that it was crystal clear in its significance. Its office was to beget in kind: with pollution and baseness, or with victory as understanding of the pure vitality was advanced. The frightful monster which has power to augment whatever is accepted is naught but the little *s*elf dwelling in fear and giving itself its own power and authority. Accepting the power of that which is preeminent in thought either enlarges the undesirable into frightfulness or, through attainment of self-mastery, reverses to calmness and beauty.

VERSE 3

And I perceived that the principal thing was to destroy or subdue the calamity of fright and then to impose impotency upon its treachery, thus reversing affliction (which is a form of division) to perfect Wholeness, through adoration of the ever-present saving power of Goodness. And all the inhabitants of cosmic perpetuity and orderly arrangement were astounded at the eternality and vitality of sheer Life.

VERSE 4

The destructive aspect of vitality is a depressive one which augments the capacity to destroy. Life is Life! Breathing after the untrue force *it* is augmented; reversing the direction of attention to breathe after freedom, self-mastery and valor, *these* capacities are augmented. Thus worship is depression or reverence, according to the capacity worshipped since the vital life force is everpresent to be directed. What can be compared to the everlasting vitality of life! The Divine Expression is arranged to appear as opposites, having the ability to advance in either direction: to create or to cut down, to enlighten or to embitter, to mass for worship or for dissension. Life is experience and experiment. Who or what opposes life save life itself? Life deprecates and shuns experiences, only to be hurt by them, or learns to know them and so becomes cleansed by and through them.

VERSE 5

And this great life-force had motion, was able to go forward or backward, to retreat or to return to the starting point, to forsake and give up or to re-store and be safe. It could initiate discipline, pondering, considering, conversing, uttering, finally acting, performing vast and mighty acts of scorn and repudiation or of Almighty Goodness, duplicating itself for good or ill, ever repairing, renewing and rebuilding.

VERSE 6

And the life-force observed a tendency to scorn, curtail and destroy goodness, to perforate the nature of goodness and its tool, the body. It tried to repudiate the reality of a state of sublime exaltation, and then, nothing was sacred to this life-force.

Chapter 13

VERSE 7

But this great vitality was earnest towards itself, and was freely permitted to select and choose either side of any undertaking; it could oppose or worship, defile or hallow. The Essence of itself was pure and perfect altogether and therefore could afford to be bent or twisted, to be used for any transition, since in reality there is only good. Strength and mastery are known only *through* knowing both sides; an "opposite" need not oppose antagonistically. Make the transition to the other side and it is revealed that the same life-force exists there, and there is *good* existing there whatever the apparent species or expression or usage:—herein is our redemption!

VERSE 8

And all that remain overwhelmed by the sense of opposition shall be depressed, worried and fearful until their natures are fired with that imaginative sense which abolishes fear and chooses the silent protection of firm substance concealed from sight, with no beginning and no ending, yet which IS the very existence, Breath and Life of Life itself—the un-namable One.

VERSE 9

Use your ears to hear, not external sounds, but what the Spirit, this One, says to *you* at the center of *your* being!

VERSE 10

That idea which shows the way to exile denudes itself and strips itself of elevation. Likewise that idea which turns inward, *re-*turns to the starting point and finds itself, finds itself as a thought arising, approaching companionship and deliverance. Thus the one which roams from the safety of truth and virtue will surely die—be destroyed by itself, while that one which cohabits with Truth *becomes* complete. He that destroys by giving up or evading his responsibilities must in turn be pushed away and neglected. This is the test of endurance, the security of assurance, the fidelity and stability of feeling, for according to the feeling, the expression is *defiled* or *hallowed*.

VERSE 11

I regarded this vital, strong aliveness, this good feeling, with great pleasure and it proclaimed a great disclosure—a veritable revelation—the exceedingly high origin of opposition. It announced that one might go forth to "survey for evil" or to "look for good." The point of decision is the pivotal point since each "creature" is free to select the journey and will in turn come upon or encounter "evil or good" in accord with each choice. The duality, thus, is double-edged—it may lift or destroy, may set upright or may level the choice. It is the strength or the weakness of the Imagination which draws one closer to Goodness or enlarges the breach, proclaiming opposites as mates, helpmates and counterparts, or as destroying, monstrous terrors.

VERSE 12

This second vitality, the vitality of choice, wielded the full privilege, the freedom and the mastery of the original; when these two vitalities are opposed they are separated and weakened; they become strengthened when they turn towards and draw near to each other: then separation vanishes in nearness to and praise of the One, and that which appears opposed becomes the counterpart, the other self which is THE SELF. This is the only, the true marriage, which heals all dis-ease and restores vitality, making safe and whole the feelings which were split and afflicted. Here is our Savior, our Realization of Oneness.

VERSE 13

Worshipping the united self increases ability and power, creates enlightenment, assures the relationship between the high state of sublime exaltation and all seeming opposition; thus the affliction of outward appearance is transmuted into an inspired appearance of Light to revere. Look well, behold, consider, discern, revere and rejoice, gaze with wonderment at the wholesomeness of the complete person—woman-man, wife-husband, dreamer-builder, mortal extended to COMPLETE MAN—DIVINITY.

VERSE 14

Uniting with opposition (which is indeed but another aspect of the Presence) enraptures the Imagination so that it weaves from ignorance, sorrow and wickedness a great understanding, knowledge and wisdom. When separation is better understood it is seen as differentiation rather than division, thus seeming oppositions complement each other to bring forth marvelous works and show the Wholeness of the Absolute One. Have respect for this living vitality, refute the darkness of opposition, see *contrast* only! Choose the divine expression of realization and say: "None of these things disturb me"! Choose the likeness and character of a healer—an exact copy of the Causative Cause—which alone makes whole after separation has been given up in a great desire to live in peace!

VERSE 15

And this great vitality was aware of its very present existence, of the highest there is—God, Divine Principle. Through this awareness the decision was made as to what should be destroyed and what healed.

VERSE 16

The just purpose of all existence (whether expressed at the moment in nobleness or pettiness, in success or destitution, in liberty or servitude) is to exalt the Self, to forgive the little self, to yield it to the High Self and so come to exist in fullness delineating absolute power, paying attention only to that which is worthy.

VERSE 17

The WHOLE state or expression alone is worthy or able to win, to surrender to or to redeem the lesser one; it IS the Savior and its signature is the nature of authority, of understanding, of utter awareness. Only this knowledge of the oneness of all things—however opposed they may seem to be—only this can ever expiate sin, sin being the sense of separation, the *dual state* whose opposite is ONE STATE—the ONE absorbing the two. This is IT—the Great and Final Authority!

VERSE 18

This is the Center of all things: to be aware of existence as *THAT* most worthy of esteem and value, as the Causative Vitality of the Logos or Divine Expression, which alone can expiate all sin (can wipe out all separation). This is the Christ of the Whole Being, of men and women, and thus of MAN; take inventory, search and find out that this basic Truth is Joyous and its gladness multiplies and increases indefinitely into myriad, endless multiples of its SELF; all are ONE.

Chapter 14

VERSE 1

And I advised myself to wait expectantly and to anticipate in thought toward good; and at once was brought forth the image and it substantiated the uplifted feeling of expiated sin which follows when "Jah has prevailed" and "Oneness" replaced duality: in this togetherness and feeling of completeness is the "mothering" state which increases indefinitely into greater abundance of the same nature or source; there is no limit—existence IS and it expresses in kind.

VERSE 2

And I was persuaded by the vibration of expansion and I yielded myself to expansion, and the undesirable dissolved away, slaking my thirst for it and satisfying me with abundance of secure desires which called aloud to me in tones of sweetest song.

VERSE 3

The purpose of this fresh song was to create change, to redirect my attention and reform my desires so that I would turn about and restore the utterance of praise. This induced a "motion towards" the place of power and an "allowing of generation" i.e. permitting to be conceived a new *life*—born *out of* desolation *through* confusion—fresh, vital, new emotion in great abundance. This new way is observed only through discipline (complete discipline of *MAN*—male and female—imagination and emotion) in order to use the Mother-Father state of creative power. Again there is no limit, either as to amount *or* direction, existence IS and IS in agreement with constant or habitual thought and feeling. Hence, to be rid of formed expression it is necessary to "about face," turn away from or release that expression; only the one who so does can find release and at-One-ment.

Revelations on The Book of Revelation

VERSE 4

Only such as find this release can avoid becoming entangled in confused emotions, for it is such an one only who is single-eyed and one-pointed in purity to Good. Hence it follows that such as do not become spoiled or wounded through their feelings or emotions are the ones who keep united secretly (or in their deep or innermost parts) with that Good. These are the ones which are joined in perfect understanding to imagination, knowing imagination to be a transition state, necessary in the moving on toward that perfect center which is the starting point to which we all must return. These who so understand and believe are rescued from recognized experience, sacrificing it for the image of Greater Good.

VERSE 5

And in their speech came forth no trickery, for they comprehended wisdom and moved toward the place of power by feeling not separate from Good.

VERSE 6

And I considered another aspect or possible message hidden in the depths of myself, in the very center of expansion, existing for the very purpose of announcing Goodness and well-being and to proclaim assurance to all who remain firm and who accept form cheerfully. This message was for wholeness of races, clans and languages—yea, for all the multitude of congregated units,

VERSE 7

and this message related, with the intelligent majesty and security of a strong vibration: "Stand in awe of and revere the power of Goodness and move consciously toward Goodness and return to your own center with praise; for it is the moment and time of and for prayer, when the Real Self will make known to the human self the sublime exaltation of their Oneness. Whether in outer form, in the roar of duality or through the vigor and energy of expression:—all, ALL are ONE"!

Chapter 14

VERSE 8

Closely impinging on this message came the opposite expression of the same one, substituting in this way: "Confusion abounds when accepted, or it may be overthrown; the use, absorption and preservation of mental excitement, *mixed with feelings*, may be directed toward or away from this confusion."

VERSE 9

And a third message or sign was boldly sounded: "If any person carves fresh vitality out of his character, exalting in his expression the HIGH SELF, clearly approaching the sense of Power,

VERSE 10

this very HIGH SELF shall absorb that which is expelled, and dissolve the angry breath into the breath of spirit (which is the origin of *all*, mixed and separate though all things may seem), thus delivering the human self from its grief and fury. All wrath and anger consume and burn, turning the anger into a touchstone, but Divine Power shines through and knits together with new enlightenment of Wholeness, uniting the seeming opposites—it takes real imagination to perceive this."

VERSE 11

Otherwise anger continues to inflict and grieve, appearing as an evil for an age, a generation or a revolution of time; there is no repose, no pause, no peace, no time to seek or to enquire nor yet to turn back and again carve the healing vitality out of the inner substance. Although whoever admits the strength and truth of this inner exalted Self—and *pays attention* to it—that one will understand the nature of this Real Self and so will draw it forth. [Over and over we are told that duality is a differentiation only; see it as a mark of and for distinctness and the power of Oneness remains. See it as a calamity, a dread, and confusing conditions, weakness and fear move in.]

VERSE 12

Therefore endurance *of this sort* makes whole (or Holy). Likewise this Real Self guards, protects and preserves the perfect order and decree of WHOLE GOODNESS and establishes the inner feeling and conviction that there is a saving power indwelling.

VERSE 13

And I paid attention to and gave heed to the vibrating inner conviction of exaltation and expansion as it laid forth reasoning and utterances about the Divine Expression within, declaring: praise or blame, cursing or honoring, destroy the one who alternates or wavers between them. It is the self-same law which responds repeatedly, yea, which gainsays or refutes the opposite as the new life is called forth; constant reversal of opinion causes flabbiness, begetting failure and keeping the self in bondage and persecuted.

VERSE 14

And I perceived that one could look for evil or survey for good, observing either good in dazzling form or evil in dark gloom (in either of which states, then, everything would appear), establishing copies to be perpetuated and to prevail in living expression, as the principal thing in one's life. This "principal thing" could be an ornament only or could refine for dedication and protection, the choice is each man's and the power of a net or snare of darkness is as great as the strength or refuge or enlightenment.

VERSE 15

Still another message came to me, originating in the sacred inner place, boldly announcing to the gloomy one "FREEDOM, with PRAISE," extolling the joy of searching after that freedom and gathering it in and so returning to close association with Goodness and attaining the reward.

VERSE 16

And as one continued to gather a feeling of joy right in the midst of gloom, the gloom was dispersed and that one, extolling

Chapter 14

praise, was divorced from his alarm (or despair) and was caught up in the web of its opposite, and that opposite (which was joy) became the partner instead of gloom.

VERSE 17

The message (or messenger) which had its ORIGIN in JOY attains its great ability in the self-same exaltation of EXPANSION which exists in the WHOLE substance of the inner understanding:— IT IS THE SELF and is, therefore, the ability and the POWER to split away from the undesirable and to give refuge through the very act of gathering in JOY.

VERSE 18

Still another aspect exists in the Origin, the aspect of sacrifice, of burning of the undesirable states and of springing forward *from them*—prevailing, with assurance, unto victory, the victory of All-Mighty Goodness. This aspect sounded clear, announcing with a-shout-of-joy its freedom, it extolled the strength-of-praise and the encountering of freedom. Vehemently and with boldness this idea of sacrificing the undesirable bears fruit, it is the idea of pushing away the unwanted or cutting it off, of divorcing it in order to collect and gather together the noblest of desires (the direct opposite of that which troubles and binds). This is what must be engraved in the heart: that one must stand boldly-forth, exposing and releasing the binding idea, praising and gathering in its opposite—the idea of freedom, thus announcing completion and understanding. For everything is for benefit, or for growth, is for GOOD or ill, *ILL or good*, according to the point of view of the one accepting or rejecting.

VERSE 19

And this idea penetrated through the opposing fears and collected into completeness (or complete union) the separate parts, and ejected all opposed to GOODNESS, expelling violent passion as *stupid*, and twisting intensity from anger to a burning-MENTAL-DESIRE.

VERSE 20

This effervescence replaced the loathsome anger which was SEVERED and became as nothing, being drained of its life-force by lack of attention. But life-force existed and came forth in the new state, causing a skipping-for-joy, thus reversing the old state, anticipating the precious enjoyment as wholly satisfying and accomplishing the consecration of greater abundance of this joy, increasing into hundreds of thousands as JOY "mothers" increasing joy.

Chapter 15

VERSE 1

And I was aware of another indication of intense longing for expansion in the opposite way: an indefinite inducement to accept and use fear, concealing the wound and enjoying the predicament exceedingly and satiating the excitement of the mind.

VERSE 2

And I experienced a sense of disgrace reflecting and intermixing with waste, but yet the self was rescued from this opposition. Freedom from trouble was revealed as the vital force, with the power to heal and to bring forth a strong character—making the transition (when paid attention to) and transferring to a definite position of authority, establishing, continuing and enduring even against the persistent roar of duality reflecting the false appeal.

VERSE 3

And this enduring force is clear, and responsive to praise and desire, and it draws forth the child (or IDEA) of Goodness, praising the ability to *imagine and to bring forth*, relating that this child of Goodness is the Divine Expression (in latent form), wonderful, and abundantly able to accomplish miracles. It is a product of activity, whole or balanced in its mode of life or course of action, and is the sure foundation of *all* power, *whole*, *holy* and *perfect*.

VERSE 4

The SELF reveres the Law of Goodness and abides in its clarity; fearing the nature of Goodness brings burdens, revering it brings abundance of honor. It alone is WHOLENESS and COMPLETENESS—it alone is purely ALL. All who seem apart from or foreign to this whole-pure-Goodness shall yet be carved into likeness—out of *fear* into *reverence*—healed by the very motion-towards praise of Goodness; for, on the very instant of turning, the prayer for help adjusts and vitalizes the shining revelation of Goodness everywhere.

VERSE 5

Closely accompanying this perception, expectantly and joyfully regarding it and observant of it, the inner potentiality was restored (revitalized) and I was again able to use the Law.

VERSE 6

And this perfect message of potential ability abides in the CENTER of the SELF applying equally to defeat or destruction or to success and rebuilding, translucent and dazzling, concealing *OR* revealing the liberty so-long-awaited. This perfect message, although it CAN devastate, yet, contemplated with pleasure, it gives a vision pure as its origin. Prepare to value eagerly the determination to love it.

VERSE 7

For its vitality is fresh and strong. Returning to it—the ORIGIN—one is safe, complete, purged of all mistakes and pouring forth praise, gaining understanding of intense spiritual desire for Goodness which revives and preserves Wholeness. Splendor, truthfulness and confidence perpetuate victory when one dwells eternally in that Wholeness.

VERSE 8

And the ability to accomplish and be joyous, through this confidence, lifted up the splendor of Goodness and its strength and might; for it (Goodness) is FIRST PRINCIPLE, and nothing which breathes advances to the Center of Being without destroying disease in some measure. For the complete state of all living is made perfect through obedience to the Law of Good or "that-which-causes-to-be."

Chapter 16

VERSE 1

And I obeyed the yearning to search for this Origin or Center of ability—the Divine Expression opposing my present state. Completely induced to rearrange my thoughts I firmly made the transition to a different mode of action and so, returning to the starting point, demolished my violent opposition to Goodness and poured it (the opposition) away.

VERSE 2

Thus, returning to my starting point, I felt unified and fully freed and the undesirable disappeared. After the departure I attempted to ascend and stumbled; feeling depressed there rushed over me a great desolation and again I felt separate and thus sinful. Calamity afflicted me but I seized on my courage, which extended towards me, gazed mentally upon it, contemplated it with pleasure and it sufficed to lift again the fresh and strong vitality. As I again paid attention to it I was again healed and the adversary yielded to the healing.

VERSE 3

Duplicating that earlier inducement I again emptied and spilled forth my fears, pouring them out with shame; with the pouring I prevailed against (or overpowered) the strength of the fear (which was but an idol) and it failed, the breath going out of it.

VERSE 4

The message of all this was intensified as the separation increased, this time spilling forth the *un*desirable toward the source of cheerfulness, thus dissolving it; and I breathed security from my Center or Origin.

VERSE 5

And I understood the message of dissolving the wrong influence and substituting an opposite. Integrity, stability and truth make right and holy, they *are* the Law, they *were* the Law and they *shall be* the Law of Wholeness—*always!* THIS IS ELOHIM, the Supreme Goodness, and is the One Right. Search and examine this and resolve to expand *self* to SELF!

VERSE 6

They (people) appear able, or exist, in order to expend their life-force in agreement with the Center of desire for perfection. Expending it on fear defiles, but turning back to the starting point of Goodness and forsaking fear, Goodness is absorbed and sin is expiated.

VERSE 7

And I gave good heed to the Origin, or Center Strength, because the Law of Goodness is the whole strength; discerning this brings balance, integrity, sincerity and certainty.

VERSE 8

A new vitality delivered me from wasting my happiness and illumination, and I was able to glow with courage and to integrate myself in this new enlightenment.

VERSE 9

And courage burned in me, as an intense desire for security was conceived in me, and exposed the nature of Goodness, that inner, Real Essence which is able to bring about any transition by revealing the inevitability of defeat apart from it; and I was not sorry to turn back to true worship.

VERSE 10

Thus induced to deliver a judgment on my situation I expended energy and stood boldly forth against continued ignorance, preferring to understand and accomplish dominion. It took wearing

Chapter 16

effort which "squeezed-me-to-the-bone," but I adhered with patience and spoke for conviction,

VERSE 11

exposing as the True Cause the Goodness of exaltation and expansion as opposed to wearing effort and constraint. This caused me to turn back to my own Center and to think differently and to accept the opportunity for action and accomplishment.

VERSE 12

The myriad number of inducements gushing forth increased both my cheerfulness and my prosperity as the waters of consciousness poured over me, from the depths of me, and carried away the old fears, dissolving them again, and abundantly satisfying my deep urge for security. Confusion and disappointment, those wasting forces, were parched and dried up to permit a new course of life, a new mode of action, to become the foundation of new power and to rule surely and eternally with increased order and strength.

VERSE 13

And I discerned the intense strength in shame, its resemblance to desire and how it "skipped-about" in the manner of Spirit, attaining a degree of action which appeared inspiring and vital, but was only fearful and degrading. It was an impostor, and as such could only come to naught.

VERSE 14

For all that actively opposes the True Spirit serves to keep the human spirit in bondage, separating the human and divine (to all appearances), departing from safety and truth and increasing the ruling power of opposition, consuming integrity and gliding swiftly toward the desiccation of search for the Almighty One.

VERSE 15

But look intently, reconsider and take joy, for you may turn about! I, the Spirit, come secretly to benefit man, to guard and protect him from his weakness. Be alert and keep vigilant, associate with that which is honorable and worthy, wrap yourself around with splendor and magnificence or peradventure you will respond to emptiness and lack and become conversant with the shame of poverty! Look up, look within, that you may recover your vision and so lose confusion and re-gain respect.

VERSE 16

And the REAL SELF (or SPIRIT), the Uniting Principle, caused the two selves (the *seeming* two) to unite in and through controlling conditions and through praising the ONE, resulting in a transition from feeling opposed, to fusing together. At first it (the Spirit) seemed to hurt, to invade and attack the personal or known self; but in relaxing to the rendezvous—instead of fighting or resisting it—we overcome the feeling of battle and opposition and reveal the consuming power of enduring-in-joy which promotes true happiness leading to complete and perfect Oneness. [N.B. to Verse 16: this is the famous "Armageddon" verse: "gather" and "Armageddon" *both* mean gather, union or completeness: the other words ALL point out that opportunity to think can lead to "opposition and hurting self" OR to "praise, happiness and liberty!"]

VERSE 17

And this sense of COMPLETENESS induced me to empty myself again of undesirable states of mind and to expand into the power of ALL GOODNESS, breathing that power unconsciously but constantly unto Eternity. As I yielded to this inducement and abode in it in my thought and feeling, there was brought forth in me a renewed intent to search after the Vibration-of-Self-Existence, which originated all things and held the INIMITABLE capacity for SELF-EXPRESSION and increasing power. As I thought all this the Divine Expression or Christ-Light-of-Understanding within me asserted: No outer appearance can disturb me, for all opposition is in appearance only, and easily fuses into ONE. LET IT HAPPEN IN YOU!

Chapter 16

VERSE 18

And there were many irritating vibrations reacting in and through me, roaring and causing me to tremble in fickleness. My indecision caused upheavals, commotion and great confusion, again making me fearful, although the light of illumination continued to flash through the darkness as the Spirit continued to repeat: Reverse yourself and return to the starting point, or that Center from which all motion proceeds. Courage continued to contend in me with carnal or external inclination, this contention opposed victory, success and the abundant increase of my yearning desire for security.

VERSE 19

The severe and stupid desiccation twisted my thinking and separated my feeling until the intensity of that separateness drove me off my course into utter confusion. But even as this sought to cleave me *from* my GOOD I continued *to cleave to* my GOOD (albeit weakly), the confusion mixed my *s*elf until I *mixed in MY SELF* and again attained recollection and suggested to my own memory, quietly, the reward of moving toward Goodness with praise, retreating into the Starting point, earnestly knowing the result of dwelling in cruel opposition instead of in brave combination.

VERSE 20

And the howling, doleful nonentity bolted and vanished, revealing release and the freeness of restoration to heights which expiate any further sense of separation (sin). Eagerly seizing this discovery I attained greater comprehension, agreed with MY SELF and felt my Real Existence.

VERSE 21

There was cessation of the feeling of separateness and instead came a rising sense of acceptance, a moving toward courage; a powerful security again began to build in me, saluting me: Hail! be well as you return to your origin in exalted expansion and find yourself surrounded by WHOLENESS—WHICH IS TRUE UNTO ALL ETERNITY, HOWEVER YOU MAY DEPORT YOURSELF.

Revelations on The Book of Revelation

"Surrounding" may seem binding and hampering, in which case you will again resist and strike out, or it may be to you the support of Love and the all-encompassing security you so much desire. *Balance these two opposites*, ponder their profound effects and expose the strength of Goodness as Almighty and WHOLE—the True Cause of all things, appearing in form according to the reasoned word—thus inflicting defeat or stumbling, or increasing the Supreme Divinity and Goodness.

Chapter 17

VERSE 1

The inducement for complete union with my Originating Cause became stronger than the indefiniteness of constantly pouring out my energy aimlessly. This inducement communed in me as Divine Inspiration, it drew me into union with it, refuting the opposing argument, fervently admonishing that I respect the teaching of Wholeness—that Mighty Law—which serves for ill when worshipped as fearful but rewards with Good when worshipped as the GOODNESS. It is wise to dwell in this Wholeness, to dissolve all heaviness and quaff the living waters of joy.

VERSE 2

Let joy rule in you to purify *all* form, remain steadfast to your true Center, looking to IT, rather than to the outside, for all things! Reside permanently in this abode—it is the home of Goodness; to turn aside from this home of Goodness serves to subordinate and abase your joy, stupefying you and embittering you, and thus preserves the false idea of the outer being powerful.

VERSE 3

And this inducement transported me, released and pardoned, to the state in which a material sense of things disappeared and the great facts of existence unfolded to my vision. I perceived the true cause of all things to be established in stability, in fidelity and in integrity. This truth glowed in seed-form, predicting the character of the vitality to evolve from it as soon as it was exposed, for in the seed exists the sacred, full completeness of the principle—that Power which is SELF-CAUSATIVE.

VERSE 4

This Causative Power assumes the outward appearance of moods, decked in glory and beauty, suggested by dreams and appearing to be the lot or fate of the person to whom they come. The Power expresses them according to the mood, muddled and detestable or completely desirable.

VERSE 5

The character of the mood was clearly inscribed by the desire—this is beyond human comprehension and remains a secret. Confusion and undesirables increase as readily and abundantly as the desirables because there is ONE CAUSE ONLY and it responds, as called upon, to form all forms.

VERSE 6

It was clear that the "cause-to-be" power would respond in great abundance and pour forth constantly in keeping with the starting force, and therefore would defile, OR hallow, as a witness to that which was thought would save from the presently expressing state. As I understood this Truth more clearly I was at once amazed and stunned, was even stupefied, and sought to destroy myself; but again recovering my vision, I knew the mighty and remarkable power which resulted through experience.

VERSE 7

And the message of all this reminded me of the singular truth about *opposition*: the great secret truth of Causative Power is that the vitality and life-force carry out into appearance in perfect accord with the impulse which set them in motion. The life-force will transport into victory, ascending or descending as ordered, accumulating in line with the Principle and flowing forth into power for Good or the reverse.

VERSE 8

And this vitality or life-force existed and *does exist*—of a very truth [*not* comes from a word which "is often used to indicate: as truly as, of a truth, verily"] and should be given priority that it may restore and per*fect*. This is indeed profound and eventuates in complete freedom, or, conversely, leads to ruin and destruction;

standing sure and firm in the face of opposition, great ability and power are called forth, and strength and vitality revive the "SPIRIT-WHOLENESS" which is the sovereign beginning, concealed but eternal. Joy in this truth, let the vital life-force BE SURELY and ETERNALLY expressed henceforth, as the Goodness which IT IS!

VERSE 9

It is the Center of all intelligence and all Feeling, the Supreme Understanding, knowing its SELF and standing under all knowledge in support of Truth. This is the Foundation-Principle, sacred, full and complete, exalting all and removing all sin (sense of separation); this is the Cause of all that IS, and from this Principle flows forth all security.

VERSE 10

Completeness is the perfect sovereign. Man passes over from sedentary, immovable stubbornness via separation and suffering, by being driven off his course and becoming inefficient, by sinking down into *violent* opposition, finally accepting opposition, and by acceptance of it overwhelming it. This is true non-resistance, this unites duality into that which IS (although not seeming to be, by reason of limited vision). When permanent union is attained, ONENESS is revealed perpetually, and the transience of a worldly hour is as nothing.

VERSE 11

This Life-force, which is of a truth the WHOLE, this richness beyond even sacred perfection, disappears in ruin and is as nothing, until restored to its starting point, or Center of Being, by being released from fearful thoughts.

VERSE 12

The accumulation of power which I discerned grows surely, and grows toward the Real Self, which is the foundation of power, and activates man to express his natural and inborn valor. This great and vigorous capacity for freedom and mastery lifts the little *self*, exalting it in union with the One, till they blend into perfect Wholeness.

VERSE 13

United thus at the Creative Center, freedom and mastery shine with a great light, and vitality is able to express in courage and firmness and all effort is then successful.

VERSE 14

The Law of Laws, the sure ruling Principle *IS* that courageous effort and firm mastery deprecate grief and create enlightened images which subdue the antagonism of opposites, and raise the seeming opposites from opposing forces to the completeness of two becoming One. All who hear and obey this urge to unite, and proclaim it as the LAW, shall be accounted happy and acceptable and shall be established in complete prosperity—which indicates utter reliance on the Light of inner Realization.

VERSE 15

This Law of Laws asserted: "No outside thing can by any means hurt you. I, the Law, can influence and dissolve any situation, causing it to melt away when you cease traveling about mentally and decide to settle on the Truth. The consciousness which will do this, and abide in me, is borne along into increasing, nourishing plenty."

VERSE 16

And all this ability and power to become one's Self is vitally fresh, awaiting awareness of the truth that in opposing *self* to Goodness you but oppose *self* against *SELF*, and so prostitute or waste the vitality which is given you, given you not to pervert but to illuminate, given you not to make you desolate but that with it you may desolate your weakness and your fears—exposing them but to dismiss them and begin again. Having experienced so-called "ill" you now choose to experience only Goodness, the true human-nature, choose to remain enlightened and be drawn together for perfection.

Chapter 17

VERSE 17

Thus this Goodness will send away confusion and cause at-one-ment in that Center which is *the* Center of Understanding where Thought and FEELING meet to confirm completeness. This is the result of determination, and of an inclination to reach the conclusion, to reach the conclusion of confusion and find the perfect conclusion of joyous conception. This, indeed, is the REVELATION ascribed to the vitality in the Divine Expression which we behold in our highest dreams.

VERSE 18

It is the Cause of all things—this Vision of Perfect Light, the Noble Mother which ranks *first* as basic Principle, invisible but sure, *then* appears as result, visible and firm.

Chapter 18

VERSE 1

This Perfect Goodness is able to endure any extremity as it seeks to furnish satisfaction. Therefore vitality endures until the Divine Expression, or Christ Light of Understanding, is discerned and induces worship of the Real Being, which brings forth mighty strength and increasing dominion, and all opposition is understood with kindly wisdom and proper dignity.

VERSE 2

This inducement announces clearly the great Truth and sends forth freeing forgiveness as the means of expanding wealth which is capable of establishing new power. Steadfast to this inner vibration, the Light of Understanding remains unmoved by confusion—heavy and severe though it may be. One may seem to be "driven-off-course" and separated from Goodness, but one may overwhelm and overthrow the depression, worship the unseen Goodness and be accepted by it and thus become secure and prevail against depression and all opposing verdicts. Praise security and retain it, remain calm and assimilate peace, so complete and make perfect your Breath of Life. Watch and be on guard lest, offering less-love, you are disqualified from returning.

VERSE 3

All races forget their real wealth, which is that-which-is-under-desire, i.e. The SPIRIT, and so from their center they look out to *things* rather than remaining true and fixed *in that Center of Spirit*. Those who rule material things persuade themselves that these material things are profitable, thus they convince themselves that they are successful—but their security is enfeebled by outer luxury.

Chapter 18

VERSE 4

Pay attention to the deep inner vibration which is unmoved by any opposing appearance, which abides in that center—the Origin of Creation. Unite your forces and receive companionship, thus do you exalt the SELF, the real companion, and, rather than separate yourself from that Goodness and inflict defeat, you solidify the expression of all Goodness to acquire success.

VERSE 5

Sin—or a feeling of lack or separation from Goodness—impinges upon expansion in Goodness and distorts the expression of Goodness, rewarding like unto itself—in increased lack.

VERSE 6

Turn back and be at peace, restore yourself lest two-fold limitation repeat. Vacillation is a self-sown-crop, actively rewarding that which it practices—toil and labor. One's lot or fate exists through accomplishment—be it of joy to satisfaction or of toil to fearfulness.

VERSE 7

This vacillating state is weighty with grievous burdens, indulging *s*elf in luxurious pleasures which vex and torture one to depression, dealing out wounds and denying the True Center, substituting the appointment of desolation and dreaming of trouble.

VERSE 8

Thus defeat and calamity come to pass, breaking forth *as though* they were the self and abolishing the goal, through separation from the True SELF. Thus destitution and lamentation are experienced resulting in a motion toward waste, solidifying the infliction; for the Law of Goodness condemns *OR* esteems through SELF-EXPRESSION.

VERSE 9

The foundation of all the power in form is to be found at the Center—the focal point of everything. True to the Goodness out of which all came, preserving and manifesting that Goodness as a breathing vitality, all is wholeness and perfection. Vice versa, idolizing the outer form keeps the shell of form alive and active in luxurious expression until it encloses with searing flame and there seems to be no ESCAPE.

VERSE 10

Remote from the Center of Goodness, albeit only in thought, reverence approaches the fearful or apprehensive state and inflicts torture. Oh, that the noble longing to think clearly would awake again to guard the whole man, that he might again have respect for and consider perceptive prayer and thus see the Divine Law express to Goodness!

VERSE 11

When turned from that Center of Goodness *IT* is in opposition to you and then it is necessary to seek it out again—else will you lament and grieve as an exile; then only with renewed confidence can you redeem the former condition.

VERSE 12

Seek diligently to furnish what is needed: DETERMINATION and GREAT DESIRE. These crystallize and fuse into confidence, making firm all former dalliance or vacillation and likewise strengthening character; this, in turn, dissipates fear which is transformed into reverence.

VERSE 13

Thus refined into a state of uprightness or right understanding, so remain: firm and consecrated, protected and rested, cleansed from agitation and limitation, revitalized, to rule with joy, thus strong enough to breathe wholeness through your being and so heal and make every whit whole.

VERSE 14

This is the courage which is able to set free any experience that it may produce, or to bring into manifestation the breathing,

Chapter 18

living Spirit of Wholeness which is the true desire and the rich delight of every longing one, satisfying completely the suffering one and disclosing true liberty as the Christ, or Light of Understanding. This self-same understanding is the only perfect satisfaction acceptable to Goodness. Joyous completion is Revealed and increases more and more perfectly as Freedom is rightly valued and attained through greater and greater understanding.

VERSE 15

Seeking the highest expression of Good liberates power and abundance; continuing to revere and TRUST that Goodness, all grief and sorrow shall become remote and recede from you in direct ratio to the abiding in Trust.

VERSE 16

Oh that the Divine Expression would become so strong in me that no outer thing could ever again move me, or distress me, so mighty and so competent is the Divine Expression! I long to clarify my thinking and place such a guard over all my thoughts that confidence will return in me and continue to purge my stubbornness, removing it by refining it and by extending and developing the valuable and beloved Christ-Light-of-Understanding. LET *IT* become crystallized in me!

VERSE 17

This is the WHOLE—THE UNITED ONE; consider it well, revive and restore the wholeness state in you and power and freedom will be attained and become of such influence that all else will be absolved. Associating with the source of abundance increases the expression of Wholeness. Thoroughly occupying oneself with Goodness, duality ceases and again becomes remote and the *self* is once more "set-together-with" the SELF IN PERFECT PEACE.

VERSE 18

Shouting for joy at the regained freedom which had been obscured, oppression vanished and completion remained. Again united at the Center, I could move forth from Goodness and deny the power of its opposite. Goodness is the perfect Mother; watchfully guarding that Mother she delights to increase and reproduce herself.

VERSE 19

Discarding the Light of Principle proclaims oppression: sorrow and lamentation oppose themselves to Goodness: Oh! that the noble Mother of Thought—the True Center—would cure and make whole by adjusting existence; but it is all accomplished by *my* effort, effort which may be a struggle and therefore in vain, or effort made in cooperation with free-ness and therefore successful. Put all sense of duality in order and move ONLY from the Center of being—for that Center is valuable, excellent and esteemed, it is the ONE—the Whole. Have respect for this and the desolation of solitude or loneliness comes to naught in the WHOLENESS of the SOLITARY ONE.

VERSE 20

Exult and be exceeding glad, for Goodness is the SPIRIT of Wholeness and reveals her SELF as that which is sent with miraculous power to bring redemption when you agree with her and transfer your attention from the outer or opposing side to the INNER UNITED ONE.

VERSE 21

And a powerful inducement to do so lifted and sustained me so that I destroyed the opposing thought which had inclined me to stumble heavily. I thereafter arranged my opposing thoughts with miraculous energy and activity and placed a guard over my confusion, tearing it down till it was demolished and penetrating the sense of frustration till it was transported into a sense of confidence.

VERSE 22

And the resounding vibration sang with excellence, breathing sounds of triumph which all too often were *mis*heard as delusion and wiles. Triumph and alarm *sound* alike in noise—as an acclamation of

Chapter 18

joy or as a battle cry. Hence rumor resounded with fraud and subtly concealed the attainment of triumph, but, withal, with much difficulty, as I was listening intently for the authority of confidence.

VERSE 23

Confidence is courage and kindly wisdom, it illuminates with happiness and cheerfulness yoking together thought and feeling in radiant joy, marrying them at the Center point that they may UNITE to conceive Good only thus making complete and perfect the announcement of a return to greater confidence. But vacillating and wandering about agree with the opposition and traffic with confusion, whispering covertly to seduce all peoples and enchant them with delusions.

VERSE 24

The Life-force can be used to defile or to hallow, you may agree with delusion or agree with truth (agreeing with whichever one is in the innermost place). This agreement takes place in silence and is examined by the Holy One, the Spirit of Wholeness and Goodness and whatever is therein found is stamped and sealed for you—as ordered—and is SO EXPRESSED.

Chapter 19

VERSE 1

And following closely this reasoning and Divine Understanding I yielded to that same Spirit of Wholeness—the SELF-EXISTENT-ONE, existing equally in all races—and asserted that as this SELF-EXISTENT-ONE was eternally the same I would praise IT and IT alone as the Law of Good. When praised, the Law which delivers, protects and saves; which dignifies and favors with value, esteem and wealth; which strengthens with might and ability, with abundance and freedom; which, in short, is the dominion and vitality of Life itself, draws the praising one to Itself in complete and perfect Wholeness. ABIDE THEREIN!

VERSE 2

Abide there, in fidelity and equity, perfectly balanced to KNOW the virtue of seeing *all* but choosing unity, perceiving two sides but understanding that the two make the ONE, thus no longer prostituting energy on fear of the less-desired which does but disfigure and corrupt all forms. Idolatry becomes adultery as one continues to worship *one side* of the whole as the ONE and this results in undesirable consequences. Redeem yourself, turn again to the True One at the Center of SELF and start over, looking with trust and praise to the two as one, seeing ALL as WHOLENESS, no more "bad" and "good" but all Goodness. Thus ministering to Wholeness you approach Wholeness and obtain power from WHOLENESS.

VERSE 3

In thus approaching Wholeness lies safety and completion: refuting opposition as *opposing*; asserting the perfection of Wholeness as Divine Expression; praising the shining, clear Eternal ONE (SELF-EXISTENT and present at all times), thus causing

Chapter 19

moral recovery and resurrection continually until confidence in the True SELF brings eternal victory.

VERSE 4

And the vitality, resulting from this decision to unite, associates with abundance and embraces the opposition, accepting it with reverence and becoming healed as they fuse in marriage. Continuing together brings great power, so that no seeming opposition can disturb, for truly and of a-surety the perfect uniting of two is celebrated as Sacred Wholeness.

VERSE 5

The realization of this Sacred Wholeness manifested the vibrating power which was the Original One; able to split through fear and destroy or, being revered as ONE, to rise to vast and mighty magnificence.

VERSE 6

Yielding to this power, existence became richer and more favorable, resisting it, commotion and confusion raged. Alerted to praise the Law I rejoiced in its absolute ruling sovereignty and kept close to its dominion; I became united to it, feeling its might and strength flow through me.

VERSE 7

Fear abated and joy arose, bright and merry, making me feel well and restored to high favor, supported and united, protected and elevated. Imagination again brought forth ideas and caused activity and adjustment which would complete liberation as diligence was established.

VERSE 8

The cause of liberation grants confidence which expiates in dazzling clarity any frustration, and correctly expounds the Divine Message as consecrated and pure.

VERSE 9

This message or Divine Expression demanded adoration—impelled it—and, in turn, conferred great benefit and prosperity, declaring that the cost of uniting ideas to integrity and spirit resulted in a union which could only bring forth happiness, for Goodness is genuine Reality.

VERSE 10

And I accepted the justice of this message and in reverence prostrated my*s*elf and lo, of a very truth, I was saved and made Whole. For the ONE united me with it*S*ELF in complete union as comrade and co-heir in such close affinity and association that I existed as witness of the SAVING-power-in-dwelling. PRAISE and ADORE GOODNESS ONLY, *with* your Breath and *as* your Breath—for *IT IS* YOUR BREATH, it gives constant evidence of saving-power immanent and ready to manifest.

Of a Truth, LET IT BE!

VERSE 11

And this understanding was discerned by me, and given respect. I advised myself to consider it constantly and at once a dazzling joyousness bounded in my heart. As I continued to survey the vision and think on it I became convinced with inward certainty that this reliance upon the Christ-Light of understanding and illumination would establish security and balance. This verdict brought stability and certainty to me and strengthened justice and integrity in me. Using the Divine Law in this manner completes *ITS* purpose, and the former hostility to anything opposed to the little *s*elf is consumed, and the opposition re-appraised and admitted into the WHOLE as an integral part of ONENESS.

VERSE 12

This enlightened vision of Principle was amply competent to encircle my whole being for protection and to keep me aloof from old thoughts, and *would* do so provided I dedicated ALL my thoughts to it. The substance of my thoughts must be in character

Chapter 19

with the Basic Principle if I would engrave or inscribe its qualities deep in my comprehension, and none can so grave the SELF in me but MYSELF.

VERSE 13

This deep Truth regarding Principle was wrapped-in-swaddling-clothes, that is to say, enwrapped or hidden as a "wife"—as the deep innermost feelings—and could be so overwhelmed as to be destroyed, to all intents and purposes. Yet, always IT IS *THERE*, at the Center Point, silently awaiting recognition. This Deep Truth is the very Principle of all Goodness—GOD-IDEA—ethereal and invisible, capable of remaining obscure throughout eternity or of waxing strong and powerful in expression—IT IS ALWAYS and in ALL WAYS, whether disregarded and thus unknown, or acknowledged, accepted and seen.

VERSE 14

The resistance to this Truth persecutes piercingly but the pain *can* purify and refine and bring conformity to and understanding of the Truth; right attitude is followed by pure confidence.

VERSE 15

Confidence—seated in the deep Center of Being—speaks Truth and turns one back to his starting point: "IN THE BEGINNING—GOODNESS." This realization is the sharp sword, the freeing instrument of firm speech uttered to conquer all oppression, removing all division, subjugating them to correction and change. The support of all in life is either FEAR *of* or REVERENCE *for* this Inner Power. Fear tramples as an oppressor, crushing and robbing the effervescing life-force. Reverence crushes out the fear and turns the angry passion into ardent desire.

VERSE 16

[The thigh refers to the generative parts; the vesture to a garment *or* a WIFE, symbol of the Feeling.] The Imagination or male aspect, deeply engraving or impregnating the FEELING, or female aspect, with the understanding of the character and authority of Basic Principle, causes realization of the One Ruling Law of All Life—ETERNAL GOODNESS.

VERSE 17

And I experienced an abiding sense of endurance in a brilliant illumination of happiness. It flashed a message of cheerful clarity which announced again the Security of the Self-Existent One, extolling the need to *praise* and saying: "obscurity and dimness, or ignorance, depart when the proximity of the heart or the Center is attained. Collect and assemble your thoughts and feelings—they should be united, yoked as one, cohabiting and feasting on the mighty abundance of ALL-GOODNESS."

VERSE 18

Selecting the idea of Perfect Goodness to feast upon, all ill is dissolved and destroyed, for any ill is but profane Good, having no real existence and serving only to prostitute your inheritance. Your experience of good or ill is temporal and human, capable of twisting your courage from the exalted head to one of low rank and forcing you to extend your strength too far. As a man, *as man alone*, you *are* alone, but man is kindred to the Divine. REJOICE and praise *this* Truth, dwell in its contemplation, and power appears to liberate and to re-unite you to principle. If you be not worthy increase your worthiness, for nobility dwells in MAN.

VERSE 19

This nobility dwells as a fresh strong vitality, the foundation of power and the ruling force, opposed to perversion and carnal inclination; it is valiant and ready to convince and cleanse; it deprecates contention and confusion, preferring union and completeness to be in control and to prevail in behalf of JOY and to dwell together in active and prosperous might.

Chapter 19

VERSE 20

Sustaining this vitality, the untrue teacher (who often resembles the true one and conspires to separate you from your strength) is himself separated in a remarkable way and is defrauded and suspended while your self is exalted to SELF-HOOD and given a token of respect. Revere it, for it heals your ills and strengthens your real character into an exact copy of ITSELF. Discard and reject all else and throw yourself into the harbor or haven of true enlightenment and become refined into the Wholeness of Divinity.

VERSE 21

Let all that remains which is unlike the Divine be sacrificed, give yourself wholly to the Divine and know protection and serenity in this bright Joy, which will increase your resemblance to the Divine and restore your completeness, covering you with Joy and satisfaction and causing you to speak PRAISE.

Chapter 20

VERSE 1

This is the great message of and from the inner Center whence everything starts, Universally or Individually, from the Center, expanding OUT—OUT—endlessly; learn this that IS and bow down in wonder and amazement and LOVE (*never* be bowed down in depression):—YOU ARE, you exist and have substance and reality, not in your external appearance but in your inner life. This is the Reality which will open to you all Truth, *depthless and profound*, able to bind you through fright or to open a new channel for you to abounding joy. [N.B. Note two possible different meanings for "bottomless pit" as *italicized* in Verses 1 and 3.]

VERSE 2

Eschew your obstinate grasp on frightful visions, keep unmarried until you shall make contact with ORIGINAL Principle and divine the DIVINE, which often seems against your human will and seems to be for trouble, but is in reality accusing you of opposing *your own* good and limiting the abundance ready for you from everlasting to everlasting.

VERSE 3

Throw away the infernal privation of fear, it only *depresses and prostrates*; restrict it by your own word and "take-it-out-of-the-way" (shut). Resolutely establish the end of fear and be steadfast in opposing fear, let it enrapture and seduce you no longer but associate with and learn from the True Cause. Accompany this True Cause, include it in all your thinking and you will be free—not for an abbreviated time to come, but NOW and eternally.

VERSE 4

This is the foundation of power and I understood it and determined to remain steadfast. Justice and the Divine Law proffer the Breath of Spirit, utterly decapitating all which testifies against the Divine Expression of the Existing Inner Saving Power and the Idea of Utter Goodness. Prostrate yourself before this SELF, adore it, be enslaved by it and you will be vital and alive, strong and free. This is the unsearchable Truth, the great NO THING which is without form, embodied only in Imagination, an illusion to the unbeliever, but a Healer to the one who emulates it and releases the "all-of-form" to become One with the Wholeness of ALL. All that man *can* be is the receiver (as the expression) of the activity of Goodness. Accept the badge of servitude to *this* ALLNESS and be FREE, vital with the Breath of Spirit, regal in union, vanquished in Completeness—for AYE.

VERSE 5

Reverse the old, destroy it mentally, relax to peace, turn again to the First Cause, unite with it and cease all struggle; and out from obscurity and disease you will arise, through recovery of Spiritual Truth, to stand again—a Living Being.

VERSE 6

Curst (unlucky) and innocent or praised (lucky) and pure (unmixed) is that one who participates in union with the Law, using the Law with flattery and to snatch his own share in fear of "no more"—*or* using the Law with honorable cooperation and accepting all as endlessly good. This latter is the living spiritual way of arising, to this one double good ensues and the old way of trial and error, of "good or bad" or "good vs. bad" is terminated and this one attains self-mastery, freedom, valor and abundance of good, a capacity to *do* good under the Rule of Goodness. Hence, this one realizes the vital FIRST or "Principle" sovereign and keeps close to it until the union of completeness is his—*forever*.

VERSE 7

After constant, frequent and endless attention to and praise of Goodness the feeling of anything opposing Goodness concludes, or is finished. With this fear of other-than-good abolished, the *self* (which is satan when set up as important) is released, pardoned and utterly freed and returns to its starting point—*The* SELF: *self* surrendered to SELF, released from bondage and captured by TRUTH.

VERSE 8

Truly enumerating and evaluating the arguments for and against close association with the True Cause, any desire for living as anti-Cause or outside of Goodness disappears, and a desire to see all races enraptured by the opportunity to reverse their vacillation, to cease their roaming from safety, takes hold and transcends personal esteem or interest.

VERSE 9

Liberated from the dread of opposition one is brought into juxtaposition with perfect protection, encircled and surrounded; all opposition becomes complement, the counterpart or mate; all is guarded and drawn together, glowing and enlightened, expressing reverence, earnestly desired by all.

VERSE 10

The former deception of opposition which had so afflicted and besieged judgment was ejected and the Goodness of all was divined—a harbor of safety for all vitality. The grief of any untrue expression being recognized, a return to the untrue states vanishes from desire and a merging with the whole supersedes and continues into eternity.

VERSE 11

And I became aware of the great power of this union with the Eternal Cause, and I desired to remain in front of that power; facing it all sense of opposition vanished, all urge to expand was lifted up releasing the energy to dispense with all unlike Goodness, discovering the condition of liberation which resulted in perfect marriage or union with the Good.

Chapter 20

VERSE 12

Discerning this I subdued and destroyed the pestilence of foolish weakness, it was not worthy of increasing, nor could it remain in proximity to Goodness. The True Cause inscribed within was then observed, the True Cause which is ALL [life, vitality, desire, mind, immortality, spirit, the whole, pleasure, strength, substance]. Foolishness, which is an empty carcass striving to be the image of Goodness, is self-convicted, for it opposes Goodness and separates from the Supreme Good; failing to begin *IN* Goodness it lusts for that which it already *IS* and thus prostitutes itself in waste, making toil of joyous action.

VERSE 13

This constant duality occupied normal existence so completely as to limit life in such a way as to make it seem finished, separate and calamitous—a punishment to be escaped from rather than a joyous state to delight in. Human-kind was thus inflicted with a continual self-sown-crop of toil and bondage.

VERSE 14

The lake of fire may be a dread and fearful thing to you if you so desire, but fire is enlightening and refining and a lake is a harbor or haven. Thus I may cast out or utterly reject the pestilences, troubles and limitations, throw them into the harbor and find my boat of life lightened and safe in the harbor or haven of Love and Goodness. All things are twofold to human eyes and death may be an end or a beginning. Repeating troubles and dwelling in fear is to die again in calamity.

VERSE 15

Of a truth, yea verily, your own acceptances are the cause of all expression *in your expression!* Life is the self-same-substance however you may use it; cast it away and it hurts, live it in union with its own Goodness and it heals.

Chapter 21

VERSE 1

I observed with pleasure that reform is possible, that I might regenerate myself by driving out the presently accepted form and uniting with a changed and fresh idea; for every advance follows the abolishing of some idea and substituting a change, thus departing from the present appearance. And I ceased the burdensome acceptance of duality.

VERSE 2

So I became "Jehovah-favored" or Loved and full of Love, and I discerned the revelation of Wholeness. I awoke and thought afresh, expelling old thoughts, and was rewarded by a new sense of perfection coming to subdue depression and to do reverence to the peacefulness of Goodness—that Goodness which is balanced in the Expansion-Center and predisposed to remove all garnishing and reveal the complete and perfect "TWO-AS-ONE."

VERSE 3

And I responded and expanded to the vibration of Love, and a release of fear affirmed my joy and I became the abode of Spirit, uniting in closeness and courage and was set free, to remain firm and fast in permanent accord—*if I chose* to do so. This is possible for all races, for all folk, for Goodness is ALL THAT IS.

VERSE 4

And electing this permanent residence abolishes and destroys moaning lamentations, depressions and calamities, all affliction of outward appearance, all sense of weariness-at-work; for that which is FIRST—pure and utter Goodness—unites with all and unites all in perfect peace.

VERSE 5

Brooding over this indication of power, and reasoning on the Divine expression within, there came an utterance: "Look intently and with joy! I deprecate perversion and am ready to choose a fresh, clean selection, to recreate and regenerate vitality which shall be inscribed deeply with the Divine Expression—THE WORD OF GOODNESS. MY WORD, repeated again and again—*these* words are SPIRIT, are trustworthy and certain, are sure and sincere, balanced in equity and fidelity."

VERSE 6

And the assertion continued: "This is the creation which makes whole and complete, makes sound and beautiful: I—THE ONE—am FIRST, and I—THE ONE,—am LAST, the Original Principle and the Infinite Goal (or future reward) perpetually complete. So the future IS, even as you say *NOW* it is *THEN*; thus I AM the Principle of Finality—this is your strength and your victory for evermore. I, this Principle of all, offer, bestow and ascribe to you who long, the abundant satisfaction of knowing that the source of all supply is my BREATH, the refreshing vitality of the consciousness of the inner Divine Goodness spontaneously and freely offered as the Spiritual endowment of all citizens of heaven (dwellers in accepted expansion)."

VERSE 7

The SPIRIT urges all who desire to expand and to strengthen the inner Breath, to occupy the elevated place in thought that they may possess the perpetual quality of renewal, of re-birth in Goodness. "I AM Goodness and you shall express ME."

VERSE 8

To all who do NOT so desire, all who shiver and shudder, all who are obstinate and rebellious, all who defy me and are enraged and offensive, all who destroy and strike with bitterness, all who prostitute their energies and idolize outer things, opposing the inner secrets, practicing their wiles to cover the Truth, deceiving themselves and seeking to separate others from their Good—to all of you *I AM* a SEPARATE BEING, dividing your strength, apportioning your heritage, disuniting your thoughts and feelings so that you move in a circle of bewilderment, inflamed with anger . . . all of you shall pay double toll as you fear that which IS NOT.

VERSE 9

This message filled me with awe and there came a fuller inducement to unite with the perfect one and to pour out all fear and to stand boldly up to all which *seemed* "not good" and to announce to it: "perfection is eternal, you conceal my good to trip me, let me understand you!" thus I conversed with my*s*elf, musing and meditating on perfection, and the Inner Christ-Light of Understanding drew near and revealed the perfect efficiency of uniting Thought and Feeling under Goodness. This marriage results in Goodness expressing (or vice versa, for the Law itself is immutable and works to bring forth issue like unto the parent Thought and Feeling which combined).

VERSE 10

Transported by this revelation to realize the abundant power in Spirit, I again determined to raise my vision, to elevate my thought and feeling and ascend to the pure source—the Holy Mother or source of WHOLENESS—which alone is perfect and able *to make good* all things. For only Goodness can go up or down and still remain Good and capable of expanding into Greater Good. [In other words there is no "UP or DOWN" or "GOOD or BAD" but only *PURE GOODNESS*, expressing as YOU—each one of you—decree AT or IN your "staring point," THE CHURCH. (see Chap. 1, V. 11)]

VERSE 11

This revelation exists in splendor and expresses through praise—praise at the *center* of your being; this is the point of resemblance, the place where you are "likest GOD." Here is where the verdict is rendered, for equal value is given *OUT* based on that

Chapter 21

which is given (or put) *IN*: liberty for license or liberty for true freedom . . . let it be radiant and magnificent, clean and pure.

VERSE 12

Jerusalem, the friendly, peaceful and complete state, is fortified by increased learning. Learn of Goodness and by associating WITH Goodness [there are twelve gates and there were twelve disciples: twelve means to "associate with," hence, to learn from and bring forth; gate means to "estimate, to think, to deliver"; thus associate with your qualities, your characteristics and with your Supreme Teacher; learn of and from that perfect Goodness, think clearly and "good-ly" and Goodness will deliver of itself; twelve angels would be inducements to learn], learn the nature of Goodness, learn to know its character, be sure of and understand pure-goodness (this is the Holy or Whole Mother). This is engraved deep in your own heart—this nature of Goodness, associate with THIS, it is the support of LIFE (tribes) and the only complete quality which can prevail if you would become, or *desire* to become, radiantly intelligent and powerful and able to rule AS or WITH Goodness.

VERSE 13

[Three signifies "intensity": gates are to "estimate, think or deliver": west is the symbol of the "outer or external," east of the "inner or eternal": north of the "gloomy or dark": south of "a barren desert."] Thus: Through whichever thought you go, the type of thought is delivered to you in expression—intensified.

VERSE 14

[One meaning of *wall* is "to produce from seed, as a mother:" one meaning of *city* is "to estimate or think: a Mother."] Thinking *into* Feeling is the prerequisite of manifesting; this lesson *must* be learned, easily or through travail, but inculcated into your being it must be! How it is learned establishes your character and your awareness, your knowledge and your understanding. The apostle of the Lamb is HE—the Christ-Light of Understanding—that is sent you THROUGH your thinking.

Revelations on The Book of Revelation

VERSE 15

[Talked means "something said, including the thought: by implication the Divine Expression": thus we have a re-iteration of the last sentence.] This Divine Expression speaks to me *through* my thinking. Eagerly I carved or etched the thought into my determination, that I might erect or procure redemption by extending my thought into the feeling or Mother-nature, and by guarding and enclosing my thoughts, restrain them and thus "produce-seed-as-a-mother" (wall) and so deliver the desired expression.

VERSE 16

This exactness of delivery is protected by the coming together of thought and feeling—the solid or four-square foundation for the future posterity of revived liberty. Extending this exactness the inculcation is increased and the lesson of what constitutes redemption is fixed in consciousness and learned, securing the future, elevating and extolling dignity and power, widening the liberty. These are and must be balanced for rectitude, for prosperity and for concord.

VERSE 17

[Cubit, wall and hundred each trace back to "Mother: as bond of family: as unit of measure: as producing seed"; according is "self-sown-crop" or "that which groweth of its own accord"; MAN is "HE THAT HATH IT, vitality, breathing creature, THE WHOLE"; angel is a "message or messenger, an inducement, to bring glad tidings."] Thus: The whole message of good tidings is induced to come forth as vitality, as the Living Breathing Creature of the Self that is THE SELF—sown or produced out of its own nature as the only bond or uniting force.

VERSE 18

The creative force which fortifies the producer of seed, or the feeling nature, heals and liberates, bringing about salvation which is acceptable and desirable and which reflects happiness and resembles the *unmixed*, refined liberty found only in the Holy ONE (the WHOLE ONE).

VERSE 19

This strong basis for fortifying and establishing true conception brings about the proper order for rising to completeness, from the "sentence of human law to the verdict of Divine Law." This development is the most honored, esteemed, beloved and valued verdict obtainable and will acquit all from death. Collect your thoughts and unite with this conception, ordained from the beginning and able to deliver you into safety and freedom. Declare this truth over and over, recount and celebrate it, intensify it till it becomes a chasm of shining strength to keep you from returning to the old ways.

VERSE 20

In order to "make yourself," to accumulate great things and grow rich as the complete and Sacred One it is necessary to overcome sedentary ways, to annihilate large numbers of things and so pass over into the cheerful, bright state of rejoicing, which teaches that your dream of Power is the gem or base of all dreams which can furnish all that is needed to get you across the gulf of FEAR, that you may find your relationship *to* or *with* the FATHER-ALL-GOODNESS—THE WHOLE ONE.

VERSE 21

Thinking deeply brings about a crystallization of the thought which completes or makes perfect *whatever* is thought about. Great intensity in the thought commits one to forming the thought, which is repeated, unless reversed. Face this truth and sever your thought from the undesirable that you may express unmixed JOY and FREEDOM, otherwise they remain inaccessible for the *EX*pression must reflect the *IM*pression or that which underlies it. Thus the thought shines in the face and in the deed.

Revelations on The Book of Revelation

VERSE 22

Ability which is used for vanity, or for a vain thing, or for an act of no value, fails, for true power lies in the Law of Good. Use the strength of your Imagination on the glory and might of Goodness and your capacity to express good increases abundantly.

VERSE 23

Awake to your lack of happiness; your failure to repair, rebuild and renew happiness lies at the Center of your Being for it is THERE that your Thought meets your Feeling, THERE where you excogitate and radiate your thought into enlightened cheer or distraught rage. Value dignity and praise, imagine in line with Goodness, let the illumination of JOY break forth!

VERSE 24

This Joy heals the life of all who accept it so that they become cured and perfectly whole in the Divine Expression or Christ-Light of Understanding, the brightness and illumination of which cannot be described. The intensity of this power, when IT is ruling, accomplishes much of rare value, beauty and majesty.

VERSE 25

To think exactly and in a guarded way shall of a truth never be prohibited or restrained; all are free to use thought earnestly and diligently or to twist it into adversity.

VERSE 26

Practicing praise and reverence of Goodness in thinking produces the Life of Serenity and Harmony.

VERSE 27

And no other mode of action or course of life attains equal progress nor is any other way instrumental in finding the REAL Origin. The vital CHRIST-FORCE dissolves all other force, any idolatrous or unclean thought or disappointment fails when the message of active Goodness makes glad or rejoices the heart. Let this Pure-Goodness, the SPIRIT OF PERFECT WHOLENESS, breathe

Chapter 21

through your Imagination, causing revelation, revival and resurrection!

Chapter 22

VERSE 1

This is the Spirit which admonishes, exemplifies, instructs and discloses to you the freedom and joy to be found in ITS support. Flowing together with IT you find strength, cheerfulness and prosperity; ITS influence satisfies abundantly and utterly destroys all raw or unhappy conditions. IT is the very BREATH of your being. ITS substance is the SELF-SAME substance *as you*, IT is your consciousness, your Divinity. Value IT as magnificent, radiant, glorious beyond description, transparent in ITS Goodness, the very source of your own Origin—your ALL—the foundation of the Power in your Imaginings.

VERSE 2

This nearness or center of you participates in your desire, gathers together all of your dual longings and transmutes them, changing the direction of your longings as *you* alter your thought toward IT. IT strengthens and makes firm your existence in *Good*—bringing alive your whole Being, that Vital Principle that is your Center and that is ready to teach you and produce in you the abundant life. IT is Absolute and always at hand, ready to persuade you to rebuild and renew yourself into your complete and perfect SELF. IT will sprout in your heart to deliver, release and heal you, as you give IT your attention: IT IS THE WHOLE, DIVINE and PERFECT Life-Force of Saving Power—IT IS GOODNESS and IS *YOUR ALL.*

VERSE 3

Placing all your confidence in this Inner Spirit there will be a cessation of all maligning, of all contempt and execration, no more speaking evil; for the place of power in you will bring forth

Chapter 22

Goodness, compelling your attention and contributing to you, as to a child, *bondage* or *freedom* as you imagine *one* or the *other*.

VERSE 4

Dreaming on this aspect of Goodness, understanding it, character develops clear and strong in direct causal relationship to Goodness, and LO, Goodness is clearly discerned in your countenance.

VERSE 5

It will not be *necessary* to turn back to the old way, although failing to keep the Light white and serviceable, the Light will again become of no value; failure to shine clear or to give forth happiness augments the lack; being constantly vigilant in keeping close to the starting Center is the *only* way to have union with this Power of Goodness and to hold your Imagination in line with Goodness—until all that seems unrelated to Goodness shall vanish and you will dwell in the ETERNAL GOOD, confidently and constantly until you are every WHIT WHOLE.

VERSE 6

This assertion is certain, is trustworthy and is your deepest security, put all your reliance on this INNER CHRIST-LIGHT of Understanding. IT is the ONLY REALITY, remain firmly established there and you will find your balance. This is the REVELATION of INSPIRED and IN-BREATHING LIGHT which will divorce you from the outer and release your inner aspect, or messenger of Good News. Declare your whole attention to be upon Goodness, live according to that Goodness and IT will compel the Divine Expression to be elevated in you, for IT IS at hand, sound and beautiful, ready to save you from all injury.

VERSE 7

Advise yourself well; respect this vision and it will be attained speedily and completely, keep in the straight way, associate only with Praise and your Good Desire lifted into acceptance will be the cause of Goodness expressing.

VERSE 8

The SELF-EXISTENT-ONE within me discerned with awareness the very astonishing Light of Christ Understanding, the True Realization, from which I had seemed separated and so driven off my course. I had stumbled and fallen but now I bent in obeisance and yielded myself to utter acceptance, worshipping with my whole attention and in complete reverence, being healed. As I neared the Center, with praise, I was set upright to delineate or suggest support and to reveal victory.

VERSE 9

This SELF-EXISTENT-ONE, which opposed my fears, asserted the Presence of Christ-Light-Understanding-in-me and said: Look up! Look within! Regard this with joy and practice no other work as assiduously as you serve this Realization of Understanding. Practice humanly and practice divinely, that the *two* may be *ONE* in you as a companion and close associate, participating to unite the human and the divine into the Christ WHOLENESS, as agreed upon for your protection. Celebrate this declaration by your word of acceptance and it becomes the cause of healing and of increased nobility.

VERSE 10

Do not oppose these things in your heart but rather intensify your attestation of them as deep mental desires, accept them and sing for joy and you will be lifted up, do not procrastinate! If *you will approach this truth* NOW the Original Cause will move through you—as a channel—to cause a festival of re-commencement, a beginning again for ETERNITY.

VERSE 11

If any one has not yet reached the safety of completion, of perfect prosperity, of pleasant and friendly virtue, let him forgive the

Chapter 22

lack and relax in quietness, repose in peacefulness and persevere in seeking his Center. Release those that seem depraved, commend and praise *the-good-in-them* and abide with them. Using this power as far as in you lies, continue to avoid worry and endure in calmness, then shall you return to the Pure, Whole and Vital Principle.

VERSE 12

Consider this joyfully and attain the desired vision without delay, for the recompense or reward restores peace. Turn back and be at peace as you reunite at the Center with the One who will become known only as you persevere earnestly and diligently.

VERSE 13

This One is the Only Cause. IT images, IT sets in motion and changes the old image and IT becomes the new. IT IS the Vital Principle, *First* in Time, Order and Rank, IT IS BEFORE THE FIRST, FOR IT ORIGINATED FIRST, MIDDLE AND LAST, IT IS COMMENCEMENT AND FINALITY—REPEATED ENDLESSLY—"and of this kingdom (this foundation of power) there shall be no end." IT IS INFINITE. IT SEEMS TO BE MANY, yet IT is united, for IT IS ALL AND IT IS ETERNAL!

VERSE 14

Adore the Order of this One and the Order of ITS Decree, practice integrity and gain strength and firmness therein, for integrity is the substance of ALL GOOD. Guard well your thought and your feeling and let them move only in the direction of your Original Good—the HIGHEST GOOD IN THE UNIVERSE.

VERSE 15

As long as you prostitute your Imagination, desolation will separate you from your Good, whispering magical enchantments to cover your wisdom with "spells," to make idolatry seem sanctified, to cast forth and destroy by antagonistic opposition; all this as long as you cling to and choose travesty, hypocrisy and sham.

Revelations on The Book of Revelation

VERSE 16

I—THE SPIRIT OF YOUR OWN INNER-SAVING-POWER, THE SELF THAT EXISTS *IN* the *self*—I release this message in order to restore your attention and to repeat and corroborate the inducement which shall cause you again to think clearly, again to think of the Divine Christ-Light of Understanding which unites Thought and Feeling at the Center of your Being from which all action starts. I, this TRUE SELF, *AM* and I AM the very Center from which all action starts. I AM also the product of Love made *stable* in your Center through clear perception and Radiant Joy.

VERSE 17

This very Breath of Life at your Center IS that ONE which completes and makes perfect by THINKING *into* FEELING, thus Impregnating the Receptive with, by and through the Active, thus bringing forth that which IS ETERNALLY. Surrender any sense of yearning, absolve the *longing hope* which *half doubts*, and determine to be *sure*, to *know* that I AM YOUR REAL SELF! Resolve to lift your *self* to ME and to follow closely, capturing and maintaining the conception of Consciousness as "THAT WHICH IS"—as that which expresses in vitality the Spirit as it is accepted. This is the freedom of Spiritual Endowment—that IT IS THE EXPRESSION OF ITS OWN IMPRESSION.

VERSE 18

This reality announces that any person is "he-that-hath-IT," for to exist at all is to have the WHOLENESS—is to "BE WHOLE." Do not neglect this Divine Idea announced to all, pay attention to it and sing about it! Ponder *on* and expand *into* this Truth—IT IS YOUR DEEP DESIRE which can lift you, surging through you as inspiration, the Breath of Goodness, to cause all things. If, however, you scrape or shave this Truth, scattering it and imposing your little-*self* ideas upon it, you ruin ITS INTENT and the Law of Goodness can only increase the ruin (since the idea of ruin has become your purpose) and so defeat your real intent.

Chapter 22

VERSE 19

Anytime that "HE-THAT-HATH-IT" (which is *every one*) shall eschew his SELF, and divorce himself from that SELF, the idea of divorce becomes a burden, causing the Law of Goodness to sustain the accepted idea of lack and limitation and to remove the feeling of Oneness with the Center or Origin or Father-Cause. The Breath of Spirit is the WHOLE, guard this Vital Truth, awake to it, grave it deep within; the Law of Good is all that there is and IT always supplies that which you sustain in your mind and heart, your Thought and Feeling. Unite these two in Joy, regard the WHOLENESS of Good as ever present or if your needs must unite them in doubt and fear, be not put out when these things (doubt and fear) express and increase—they are your demand and therefore must, *in Law*, be expressed.

VERSE 20

Pay attention to and respond to this report and hereafter follow the Divine Expression of Christ-Light . . . UNDERSTANDING. Refute and deny the power of any antagonist to GOOD! Truth is steadfast and unshakable, it comes to pass easily and in certainty, a covenant of the Law, it comes without delay, is dependable, supporting that which is urged upon it. Limitation is expressed equally with freedom according to the strength of the attention upon one *OR* the other. This is SURE: yea verily, the Law-of-the-Saving-Power EXISTS! IT IS AND IT IS SURE.

VERSE 21

Joyously grateful we accept this simple truth: reflecting on the Divine, IT Expresses easily, beautifully and graciously. We give thanks for THE LAW. Let *REALIZATION OF IT* be made firm in joyous freedom!

SO IT IS. *HE WILL SAVE.*

END
Begun Jan. 26, 1945—Finished July 26, 1952.

Biography

The author was born in Brooklyn, New York, on January 26, 1897 and passed on in Winter Park, Florida, on January 15, 1987. Everything about Winifred MacCardell Flood says she lived a lively and vibrant life. From accidentally starting the first sorority at Rollins College (attended 1915-18) to giving public readings of prose and poetry, "Tiny" lived large. In 1921 she married Frank MacCardell, a doctor, with whom she had a son, Cameron, in 1929. From there she went on to study metaphysics in New York City, which ultimately resulted in her ordination as a minister.

The author married her second husband, Paul Flood, an opera singer, in 1948, and they moved to Winter Park, Florida, in 1952. There, she and Flood had a studio where together they taught public speaking in the 1950s and 1960s. MacCardell Flood also gave what she called "Truth Talks." In these it appears that she invited her listeners to consider the foundations of reality and the awakening of Man to his divine nature, as she also does in this book. She completed another book/pamphlet, *Ten Messages for Joyous Living: An Interpretation of the Ten Commandments*, in 1956.

www.ingramcontent.com/pod-product-compliance
Lightning Source LLC
Chambersburg PA
CBHW052027290426
44112CB00014B/2408